Acclaim for

THE GAMING MIND

THE GAMING MIND

THE
GAMING MIND

A New Psychology of
Videogames and the Power of Play

ALEXANDER KRISS, PhD

THE EXPERIMENT

NEW YORK

THE GAMING MIND: *A New Psychology of Videogames and the Power of Play*

Copyright © 2019, 2020 by Alexander Kriss

Originally published in Great Britain as *Universal Play* by Robinson, an imprint of Little, Brown Book Group, in 2019. First published in North America in revised form by The Experiment, LLC, in 2020.

The Experiment, LLC
220 East 23rd Street, Suite 600
New York, NY 10010-4658
theexperimentpublishing.com

This book contains the opinions and ideas of its author. It is intended to provide helpful and informative material on the subjects addressed in the book. It is sold with the understanding that the author and publisher are not engaged in rendering medical, health, or any other kind of personal professional services in the book. The author and publisher specifically disclaim all responsibility for any liability, loss, or risk—personal or otherwise—that is incurred as a consequence, directly or indirectly, of the use and application of any of the contents of this book.

THE EXPERIMENT and its colophon are registered trademarks of The Experiment, LLC. Many of the designations used by manufacturers and sellers to distinguish their products are claimed as trademarks. Where those designations appear in this book and The Experiment was aware of a trademark claim, the designations have been capitalized.

The Experiment's books are available at special discounts when purchased in bulk for premiums and sales promotions as well as for fund-raising or educational use. For details, contact us at info@theexperimentpublishing.com.

Library of Congress Cataloging-in-Publication Data available upon request

ISBN 978-1-61519-681-4
Ebook ISBN 978-1-61519-682-1

Cover design by Beth Bugler
Text design by Jack Dunnington
Cover images by diversepixel/Shutterstock.com
Author photograph by Dawn Kriss

Manufactured in the United States of America

First printing March 2020
10 9 8 7 6 5 4 3 2 1

For my parents, who taught me the value of play,
and my son, whom I hope to teach.

It is play that is the universal and that belongs to health: playing facilitates growth and therefore health; playing leads into group relationships; playing can be a form of communication in psychotherapy. . . . [The] natural thing is playing.
—D. W. Winnicott, *Playing and Reality*

Contents

Author's Note

THIS BOOK CENTERS on two things that are hard to talk about, that we often feel we're not supposed to talk about: videogames and psychotherapy. In the interest of defanging these topics, I want to make clear from the start some of my choices, specifically the use of certain terms and my stance on confidentiality.

Unless otherwise noted, "game" should be regarded as synonymous with "videogame," itself an anachronistic term that has never been properly revised. In discussing individuals, the term "gamer" is used only in particular circumstances, as it carries an emotional and political charge levied in some circles as a derogation and in others as a proud self-designation. I prefer the term "player" to more broadly (and accurately) describe a person interacting with a game.

This book includes several descriptions of psychotherapy. One broad reason for doing so, in my view, is to demystify the process and demonstrate how treatment can serve as a safe, supportive environment to help people work through various issues. At the same time, it is important that educating the reader does not come at the expense of confidentiality, for the sake of the individuals described as well as anyone who might be considering treatment but has concerns about trusting a professional to treat their innermost thoughts and feelings with care and respect.

I have attempted to responsibly walk the line between representing psychotherapy authentically while protecting the identities of those discussed. The cases herein are all based on real people with whom I have worked, but their names and other biographical details have been altered significantly, and in some instances the themes from two or more treatments were combined into a composite case. In my private practice, I always obtain written consent from patients to include aspects of their treatment in my writing, on the condition that confidentiality is not breached. I take few things more seriously than the privacy of psychotherapy and want any reader of this book to be assured that my intention is to illuminate and never to exploit.

Chapter 1

Me, You, and *Silent Hill 2*

What do the games we play, and how we play them, say about who we are?

What an abyss of uncertainty, whenever the mind feels overtaken by itself; when it, the seeker, is at the same time the dark region through which it must go seeking and where all its equipment will avail it nothing.

—Marcel Proust, *Swann's Way*

"BASICALLY," SHE SAID, "he's a gamer kid. You know?" Everyone nodded: they knew.

I sat in a weekly staff meeting at the outpatient clinic where I worked as a graduate student in clinical psychology. The chief purpose of the meeting was to present the team with new cases coming into the clinic so we could decide what treatment and potentially which therapist would be most appropriate to meet their needs. A few moments earlier, a colleague across from me had begun to discuss a young man she'd recently interviewed for the first time. He was twenty-one years old, living at home with his parents and siblings, enrolled in college but struggling. Then, while describing the specific circumstances of this man's life, she paused, then winced, like there was an idea in her mind that she couldn't quite put into words. "Gamer kid."

It was the way she said it. Not with malice or contempt, but indifference. She and I worked together in the field of understanding, yet she presented "gamer kid" as a concept that merited no scrutiny; she was saving us valuable time, we all knew what she meant, let's just move on already. As though this phrase, or any phrase, could sum up an individual's character. I felt unsettled particularly because this was not how I expected my colleague to behave. If an insensitive clinician speaks insensitively it would be upsetting yet easy to quantify, but I'd known this woman for many months and had come to admire her natural compassion and curiosity, which to my mind represented the ideal characteristics of a psychotherapist. How could she speak of this young man so dismissively?

"Sorry," I interjected, unsure whether I wanted to convey offence or remorse. "I don't think I know what you mean."

She must have detected my prickliness as she dropped the colloquialism and dived into professional jargon, also unusual for her: "I mean that he lacks the basic interpersonal skills that would be developmentally appropriate for his age. He doesn't have relationships or hobbies to speak of and he's barely getting by in school. All he really does is play videogames."

"But . . . what does he play?"

Everyone around the table—an impressive collection of psychologists, psychiatrists, social workers, and trainees—looked at me blankly. They knew me as someone unlikely to eat up time in meetings with inane questions, yet no one could see what I was driving at. What difference did it make what he plays? Even I didn't know exactly what my point was or what it was that I was trying to make the others understand.

But something was unraveling inside me: a knot of emotion, a

part of myself far removed from my identity as a grown-up professional. Images flashed before my eyes, old feelings rose up, familiar
and alien, all at once—I felt on the verge of crying out. Proust
once wrote of a tea-soaked madeleine that, upon touching his
tongue, transported him instantly to a childhood long obscured
by the haze of the past. "Gamer kid," that callous phrase, was my
madeleine, the unexpected trigger rocketing me back in time to
dormant memories turned newly vivid.

WHEN I WAS FIVE YEARS OLD I had a pig called Hen Wen.

She was an unusual pet, to be sure. Though small—measuring
no more than a few pink pixels in length—Hen Wen possessed
clairvoyant abilities sought by the diabolical Horned King and, as
her caregiver, it was my responsibility to keep her safe. My father
shared the burden with me, to some extent, as the two of us played
Sierra On-Line's 1986 game *The Black Cauldron*[1] together on the
IBM AT he kept in his basement home office.

My access to this virtual world was an unusual privilege I didn't
yet appreciate. My father's employer had furnished the powerful
computer we used at a time when most families, if they owned
a home computer at all, were forced to settle for the cheaper but
vastly inferior Apple IIe. Babbage's, one of the first retail outlets
to sell videogames to consumers in the US, happened to have
opened one of its first locations a few streets from my father's
office in downtown Boston, Massachusetts, and my father happened to be friends with the owner. When he asked this friend
to recommend something fun he might do with his son on the
computer—the son who had shown markedly less interest in organized physical activity than his older brother—the friend suggested we give *The Black Cauldron* a try.

"Fun" would be a gross understatement; the game mesmerized me. The visuals were sophisticated for the time, though the graphics were blocky and the color palette limited, but the chief appeal was the suggestion that my decisions had a meaningful impact on the world. The player, inhabiting the role of a humble farmhand called Taran, had to lead Hen Wen to safe haven. In the book or film version—both of which predated the game, though I had heard of neither—Hen Wen's capture by the Horned King's minions represented the dramatic incident that catalyzed the rest of the story. But in the game this trajectory was not wholly determined by author or director: instead, branching possibilities were designed to accommodate the actions of the player. If my father and I raced fast enough from the starting screen of Taran's farm to the well-hidden refuge of the Fair Folk several screens away, Hen Wen could be safe for the rest of the game. If not, we would endeavor to rescue her and risk the possibility of her death in the process.

For a young child, the idea that actions have consequences is developmentally novel, filled with excitement and anxiety. My father—whose superior dexterity at the keyboard demanded that he take direct control of Taran while I barked instructions from his lap—must have been maddened to tears when I asked him to play and replay the opening sequence. Sometimes we skirted disaster and delivered Hen Wen to safety. Other times we were too slow or forgot the way or Taran snagged unfairly on a pixelated bush and a winged beast appeared on the screen along with a box of text ("Oh no, it's one of the Horned King's evil gwythaints!"[1]) to carry Hen Wen off in its clutches.

Those afternoons on my father's lap represent my earliest memories of feeling as if my choices mattered and provided my first glimpse of the complex emotional landscape that defines human psychology. The risk of losing Hen Wen was both terrifying and thrilling. Her capture filled me with worry for her safety as well as guilt over that preceding thrill and anger at my father's maladroitness at the keyboard. Likewise, a successful rescue involved not only relief and pride but also a dim awareness that it was really my father, not I, who deserved the credit.

I WAS SEVEN YEARS OLD when I nearly had a panic attack while playing *The Legend of Kyrandia*. The game, a natural descendent of titles like *The Black Cauldron*, was a story-based adventure in which the player had to solve puzzles and interact with other characters in order to advance the plot. My father still sat beside me—though I took control of the mouse and keyboard a little more often by this point—and I continued to delight in testing out the consequences of my in-game actions. *Kyrandia* seemed to share my glee in subjecting the player's character, Brandon, to a trial-and-error approach, as doing so often resulted in his outlandishly graphic demise. As my father and I neared the end of the game, I'd already led Brandon to plummet off a bridge, succumb to snake venom, be devoured by red-eyed creatures in a pitch-black cavern, burn alive, be devoured by a giant frog—and burn alive again. We were now in the castle held by the game's villain, the demented court jester Malcolm, when Brandon encountered a friend, Herman, possessed by Malcolm's dark magic. The possession was made clear by Herman's sickly green pallor and he loomed menacingly with a hacksaw in hand, one that Brandon had lent him earlier in the game.

"Brandon," Herman cried, "I have your saw!" Later versions of the game would feature actors performing the voices, but our copy only displayed the dialogue as text, which my father read aloud in a gravelly voice to indicate Herman's altered state.

"That's OK, Herman," Brandon replied. "You can keep it."

"But I sharpened it just for you!"[2]

An electric current shot through my body. Something about this tableau—a gentle soul twisted by madness, turned against me—unsettled me in a way that depictions of poison or immolation had not.

Depending on the player's action, Brandon could restore his friend to a lucid state, but not knowing what to do I charged forward, which prompted Herman to saw Brandon in half and bring up the familiar "Game over" screen. It read, simply: "Rest in peace, Brandon."[3]

The consequence of this choice felt too great. There were machinations at work within me that I did not fully understand, but it was clear that I'd struck upon a scenario too volatile to be safely contained within the unreality of the game. My father reflexively reloaded our last saved state, returning us to shortly before the dreaded encounter with Herman. I grew anxious and fretful, squirming in my chair and averting my eyes from the screen; I moaned slightly out of a developing sense of nausea. My father looked down, saw my distress and promptly turned off the computer monitor.

A YEAR LATER, when I was eight, my father and I poured hours upon hours into *Myst*, a game about exploring abandoned islands strewn with esoteric puzzles. Through a first-person perspective, the player began on a dock with no instruction and found that by clicking on the screen he could move through the vividly realized world and interact with objects within it. As secrets were discovered and puzzles solved, passageways to new island worlds opened.

Myst was an apex of bonding for my father and me. The game's slow pace and minimal guidance meant we would spend nearly as much time discussing possible solutions as actually sitting in front of the computer.

"Have we tried counting all the switch-boxes on the island?" my father might ask me across the breakfast table. My mother would eye us like we were speaking in a foreign language.

"Maybe *that's* the number we're supposed to put in the stairway panel!" I'd reply. Then we would race to the basement to put our theory to the test. Cheating in the pre-internet age was expensive, requiring either the purchase of hint books or the use of telephone tip lines that charged ninety-five cents per minute. As a result, progressing through *Myst* demanded slow, collaborative experimentation, my father and I drawing on our years of puzzle-based game experience in order to unlock the mysteries of this most enigmatic title.

My excitement was magnified by the fact that *Myst* was a runaway hit—from its release, it would hold the title of best-selling PC game in history for the next nine years[4]—which meant that several of my classmates were also playing it. Up to this point I'd rarely had the opportunity to share my passion with friends. I might have occasionally gone to my friend Izzy's house to watch him play *Doom,* a pioneering first-person shooter about a demon-battling space marine that required too much hand-eye coordination for me to even make it through the first level, or my pal Greg and I would team up for an hour or so in the two-player mode of *Sonic the Hedgehog 2* on his Sega Genesis. But few of my friends were as devoted to playing and discussing games as I was, and none had gravitated toward the long-form, story-based titles that so enthralled me. Games had largely remained an activity between father and son for me until now. *Myst* promised to shatter this barrier between my home and the outside world: As one of the first games to take advantage of CD-ROM technology and promising previously unimagined audio-visual wonder, it seemed that everyone I knew was clamoring for a copy. I couldn't wait to talk to them about it.

My enthusiasm proved short-lived. The first friend I approached was a girl named Jamie, who also played *Myst* on a nightly basis with her father. But when I asked her which island she was currently working through, she replied, "There's only one."

"No," I corrected, "once you solve puzzles in the first location you can go to new ones. I'm in the one that's full of treehouses, it's cool."

"Puzzles? What do you mean?"

"You know, all the stuff you do in the game, like the room with the boiler, the room with all the stars . . . Haven't you started adding pages to the books in the library?"

"Look," she said, incredulous, "I don't know what you're talking about. There are no puzzles." Then, with disdain, "*Myst* is not a *videogame*."

Many people, I would learn years later, shared Jamie's relationship with *Myst,* seeing it as a digital Zen garden to be wandered through without specific purpose or intention. Like Jamie, some didn't even realize there was anything to "do"; they were not versed in the language of games in the way my father and I were and *Myst* presented its goals in an unusually opaque manner. These un-gamelike qualities no doubt helped make *Myst* the unlikely blockbuster it became, but my exchange with Jamie also taught me that interest in a "videogame" carried unforeseen implications. This passion of mine was apparently viewed by others as radioactive, and my proximity to it therefore put me at risk of being seen as a mutant.

As I grew older, games became an increasingly private interest. *Tomb Raider*, released in 1996, marked the watershed moment when I began to play alone. I was at the onset of puberty and had the nagging sense that I didn't want to hang out with the game's bosomy protagonist, Lara Croft, with my father sitting beside me. Looking back, I can scarcely believe my gall in asking him to pay for a box emblazoned with the image of Croft in a tight shirt and cut-off shorts staring out at her intended young, male, heterosexual audience. I hold no less wonder that he agreed to it without remark. The whole procedure carried an unspoken, illicit aura; if shy of criminal, it felt as though I must at least be doing something shameful.

Once *Tomb Raider* was out of the box, my relationship with it continued to walk a line between excitement and discomfort. Croft was not the first female protagonist I'd steered through a game world (that distinction went to Zanthia from the second instalment of the *Kyrandia* series), but she was the most confusing, or perhaps I was just at a point in my life when I felt the most confused. Croft was both hyper-competent heroine and unabashed sexual object; tough warrior and the player's puppet-on-a-string. The game reveled in these juxtapositions, encouraging the veneration and destruction of Croft's body in equal measure. The player directed her from behind, admiring her figure while also unavoidably leading her to mortal doom with a regularity that suited the game's ancient, trap-ridden locales. At the player's direction, Croft could be subjected to all manner of ends, from falling into a pit of spikes to drowning in a subterranean pool, and her deaths were intimate in their specificity: graphic, often slow, occasionally humiliating, and the camera always lingered just a half-second longer than necessary before the game reloaded.

Unlike my experience of death in *The Legend of Kyrandia*, which ranged from comic delight to overwhelming horror, violence in *Tomb Raider* was inextricably tied to its omnipresent sexuality; there was a perverse thrill in watching Lara die. I wasn't the only person who connected with the game as a simulator for sexually charged aggression: *Tomb Raider*'s creator, Toby Gard, acknowledged this phenomenon years later in an interview when he stated plainly, in a bewildered tone, "People just loved killing her."[5]

At the time I was unaware that my muddled teenage instincts might be considered normal in some circles; it seemed clear to me that my relationship with *Tomb Raider* was taboo and needed to be sequestered from the prying eyes of classmates who jumped at the opportunity to ostracize one of their number. The specter of judgment from the Jamies of the world loomed larger than any actual dressing-down I endured. I'd gleaned just enough of what it might be like to bear the scarlet mark of a gamer from overheard conversations at school, offhand remarks by my older brother, insults hurled at game-loving "nerds" on popular TV shows—and so in my mind I endeavored to keep a public foot in the "normal" social world and a surreptitious one in the virtual spaces that I loved but assumed most others would not understand.

My father had certainly stopped understanding them. I didn't play games in his home office anymore. I'd graduated (or perhaps been demoted) to my own spot on the other side of the basement, dimly lit, with my computer and a tangle of consoles and controllers. Sometimes he'd walk past on his way up or down the stairs.

"What's this one?" he would ask.

"It's called *Ape Escape*," I'd reply, voice cracking.

"Uh-huh. And what's the point?"

"I mean . . . I'm this kid. And there are these apes. And they, you know. Escaped."

He would chuckle, say, "Boy, oh, boy," and then continue up or down.

I had lost the ability to communicate my fascination to him. Maybe I'd never had it or maybe I was failing to notice that his question—"What's the point?"— had grown ever more existential with each passing year. He didn't just want to know what the goal of the game was, but *What is the point, child?* For god's sake, who cared if the apes escaped or not?

My best friend from the age of twelve was Bjorn, and he was highly dismissive of videogames. An affable kid with icy blue eyes and an intrepid spirit befitting his Nordic heritage, Bjorn classified games as impediments to more worthwhile adolescent pursuits particularly the goal-to-end-all-goals which was, of course, intimate contact with girls. When hanging out at his house, which I did at least a few afternoons per week, Bjorn and I made a habit of chiding his younger brother over his obsession with *Pokémon Snap,* a tranquil Nintendo 64 game about traversing colorful ecosystems while trying to capture the clearest photographs of the elusive, fantastical creatures that hid within them.

"Why would you want to take pictures of fake monsters," Bjorn posed, inviting me to join in, "when you could have sex with a real girl?"

We were, in fact, both quite far from the prospects of sex, though by the start of high school Bjorn had "dated" multiple girls in our class, while my longest relationship to speak of was a fraught one with Lara Croft. From my point of view, then, Bjorn was the undisputed expert: If he said videogames were anathema to the fairer sex, he must know what he's talking about. My parents didn't make themselves particularly available to talk about these issues. After all, they let *Tomb Raider* into the house without the barest discussion. Sex was a blind spot for them and so I felt entirely dependent on my hormonal friend to lead the way through the morass, even as I often felt frightened and unready to explore sexuality in my life outside of games.

I showed *Tomb Raider* to Bjorn and its mélange of ways to control and abuse Croft, which he found amusing but inconsequential. The appeal of spending time with this virtual character in her virtual world was lost on him; the real world held much greater interest. Bjorn preferred to look up pictures of supermodels on the internet with me, or talk about his latest make-out session with the girl he was seeing. If an experience wasn't grounded in reality it struck him as tedious, but for me, these topics and images could feel overwhelming without the buffer of unreality, the contained fantasy I'd grown so comfortable with in games. The truth was, our afternoons spent needling Bjorn's brother typically occurred at my urging. Bjorn was always up for this pastime—a way to vent some teenage angst on a smaller, helpless target—and I probably derived some similar gratification, but secretly I liked to do this because while we teased I could watch his brother search for Pokémon in the brush, which I found soothing to the same degree I found talking about sex anxiety-provoking.

My friendship with Bjorn did not solely orbit around pubescent impulses, but there was a theme of him pushing me—in a genuine, loving way—to be normal. He tried to pique my interest in sports and exercise and liked to compose daydreams of what exotic lands we might travel to as adults, what adventures we might go on, who we might meet, all in the real world. His vision of a vibrant, social existence intoxicated me and my parents encouraged Bjorn's confident, extroverted influence on the boy they saw as their bright but awkward younger child.

Less than a month after my fourteenth birthday Bjorn committed suicide. A rumor would soon spread that he'd been diagnosed with and treated for bipolar disorder for years, a gentle soul twisted by madness. I'd never heard anything about mental illness from either him or his parents and I had no idea if it was true. Cold comfort regardless. If it were so obvious, shouldn't I have noticed?

The day after, I sat at the breakfast table staring vacantly into a bowl of cereal. My father looked at me from across the table. The same table where we once concocted solutions to a weird little game set on a bucolic island. I couldn't quite bring myself to look him in the eyes. I wonder, in that moment, did he long for the days when he could protect me by turning off a computer monitor?

A couple of years later I sat in front of a psychotherapist for the first time. The reason, from my point of view, was simple: I was fine, then my friend died, then I was not.

I was lucky to be there. Many adolescents descending into anxiety or social withdrawal languish in the care of parents struggling to comprehend what is happening and not knowing how to intervene. If there is no precedent for treatment in a family the prospect of seeking it out can seem labyrinthine and rife with stigma. But the notion of psychological ailments and therapy was more commonplace for me, as my mother was in psychoanalysis for much of my childhood and spoke often of how it had helped her. So, when signs of my emotional distress grew undeniable, the idea of seeing someone felt normal and was even encouraged. It was her former psychiatrist who referred me to the clinical psychologist I was sitting across from now. I couldn't know it then, but I would also find this helpful.

Dr. Lovett was a soft-spoken but authoritative clinician. His ageless good looks reminded me of my father, and his ability to pull ideas from one of the thousand volumes that lined the walls of his office seemed to me an intellectual superpower that I longed to possess. We talked, of course, but what resonated most in this first session was the office itself, at once clichéd (midcentury modern recliner; chaise longue for patients who, unlike me, lay down during sessions) and deeply personal (the spine of each book an insight; a pleasant, earthy smell I couldn't place). I thought, *It's so still.*

I was aware that many people recoiled at stories of psychotherapy having to last for years but, privately, I liked the idea of not being on anyone else's timeline. Lovett's approach supported this desire for something open-ended: There was no rush to "get well," no agenda to follow or homework assignments to complete. The ambiguity of an unstructured session was balanced by the firm and reassuring boundaries that Lovett established to distinguish therapy—with its focus on my subjective experience—from the other areas of adolescent life that so often demanded I adhere to the views, expectations, and schedules of others.

A few weeks later, for instance, Lovett ushered me into his office on the morning of September 11, 2001. The terrorist attacks in New York—a four-hour drive from my native Boston-area suburb—began shortly before I arrived. I'd heard about them, but

Lovett had been seeing patients and remained unaware. I told him what I knew to be going on, that I wouldn't be returning to school that day, and wondered aloud if the natural impulse to keep abreast of the news meant that we ought to reschedule the session. "Well, you're already here," he said. "I can check the news after we've finished." He added, most strikingly, "Let's try to put the outside world aside for the moment."

The weeks continued, became months. I didn't ask Lovett how his day was going at the start of an appointment and he didn't expect me to; foregoing such pleasantries felt like being unshackled from chains I hadn't realized were there. He didn't know the phantasms I conjured each week—mother, father, brother, unrequited crush, dead friend—other than through the lens of my experience, which seemed to be all that mattered to him. The outside world could wait: This was *our* world, existing however briefly in time and space.

THE SAME YEAR I started therapy, *Silent Hill 2* was released for the PlayStation 2. The original *Silent Hill*, released two years earlier, was generally seen as gaming's first work of serious psychological horror, with its sights set on existential dread over the B-movie schlock that informed earlier entries in the pantheon. Rather than centering the franchise on zombies or ghosts, the antagonist of the *Silent Hill* series was the titular town itself: Forever enshrouded in fog, it existed like a shared dream—or nightmare—somewhere outside the bounds of reality, contorting itself to mirror the psyche of each game's variously tortured protagonist. Silent Hill was a place driven by laws more emotional than Newtonian, producing impossible architecture for the player to navigate and hellish monsters to fight. *Silent Hill 2* swapped the convoluted plot of its predecessor (involving a secret cult attempting to birth an ancient god) for the purely allegorical and was all the more compelling for it.

The player controls James Sunderland, a somber man who arrives in Silent Hill after receiving a letter from his wife, Mary, who died years earlier from a terminal illness in which she asks him to meet her there. James knows it's ridiculous to expect to find Mary and yet he feels compelled by something—indefatigable love? disregard for his own life? the need to clear his conscience?—even as it becomes apparent that something is seriously wrong with the town. Shortly after the player takes control of James on Silent Hill's outskirts, he meets Angela, who is inspecting headstones in the local cemetery. "I'm kind of lost," James says, meaning it literally but also belying the depth of his lostness.

Angela seems confused by James's confusion; despite the dense fog, she explains, "there's only the one road" into Silent Hill. She also advises that James not take it, as the place seems dangerous. "I guess I don't care if it's dangerous or not," James replies flatly. "I'm going to town either way."[6] The player shares this attitude, if for different reasons: While James is determined to search for his wife regardless of potentially mortal consequences, the player is eager to discover what fresh thrills this much-anticipated sequel has to offer.

Angela discloses that she, too, has been mysteriously called to Silent Hill in search of someone, and throughout the game James's path intersects with hers. They drift through town as though entranced, enduring its horrors in the vague hope that whoever or whatever they find will repair their broken lives.

The process of actually playing the game is fairly straightforward. The player guides James through Silent Hill's eerie streets, exploring abandoned apartment buildings and hospitals, solving puzzles to unlock passage to new areas. Throughout, James is beset by gruesome, writhing monsters that he must flee from or dispatch. (He begins with nothing more than a two-by-four with a nail in it, but eventually finds more lethal weaponry.) The monsters glisten with an unnatural sheen and all have smooth, featureless faces. While the combat system is not especially interesting on its own—the player essentially presses the same button repeatedly until the enemy falls, then finishes it off with a kick to the head—the experience is made tense by the disturbing appearance and movements of the monsters and even more so by the game's suggestions that perhaps the creatures James repeatedly bludgeons to death aren't really monsters, but simply look that way to him.

The notion that one's life is dictated not by what is real but what is perceived to be real is central to *Silent Hill 2*. Whenever James's path intersects with Angela's, the player is left feeling confused and unsafe because neither can seem to agree on a shared vision of what is happening around them. Following their initial meeting in the cemetery, James next comes upon Angela in an apartment building, where he finds her lying on the floor, drearily considering a large knife she holds in her hand. The very image feels absurd, a woman draped nonchalantly across the ground as the player sits tense with controller in hand, ready for the next monster to jump out. James talks the knife out of Angela's hand through a surreal, staccato dialogue in which they seem to be talking at each other rather than actually communicating. James then half-heartedly offers to accompany Angela, suggesting they might fare better if they travel together. "I'll be OK by myself," Angela replies. "Besides, I'd just slow you down."[7] James doesn't argue the point—and the player isn't looking for a sidekick, anyway.

After a long stretch, James reconnects with Angela in their most bizarre scene, set in a maze of hallways beneath the Silent Hill Historical Society. James hears Angela cry out from a nearby room, begging her father not to hurt her. When James bursts in, he finds her cowering before an odd lump of a monster that hardly resembles a human at all. After dispatching it, James approaches Angela and the player anticipates some gratitude for his efforts. "Oh, I see," Angela says with venom in her voice, "you're trying to be nice to me, right? I know what you're up to. It's always the same. You're only after one thing."[8] She departs without any discussion of the clear disconnect between what she and James perceived to be happening in the room.

The wrenching final meeting between James and Angela occurs near the end of the game, with the two standing on a grand hotel stairway that is inexplicably on fire. It is clear that Angela is beyond saving at this point and also that James has never really understood her plight. James—and, by extension, the player—has been too distracted with his own mission to recognize Angela's ensnarement in the loop of her past abuse; his commitment to a singular view of the world has foreclosed any meaningful effort to steer Angela toward a healthier path. Or was that even an option? Hadn't she established from the outset that "there's only the one road"? The mood is somber; James and player both want to believe that salvation is still possible for *them*, that they are somehow playing a different game than Angela, but the doubts are creeping in.

"It's hot as hell in here," James says, not knowing what else to say. Angela glances at the flames licking the banisters on either side.

"You see it, too?" she asks with mild surprise. "For me, it's always like this."[9]

She confirms the player's suspicion that each person experiences the horror of Silent Hill differently. Only for this brief moment are James and Angela living in the same reality, truly sharing the same time and space. Then she walks away.

I became obsessed with *Silent Hill 2*. I played its twelve-hour runtime back-to-back, probably a dozen times. I discussed it exhaustively on message boards behind the veil of online anonymity—never with friends or family. Never even with Lovett, the one person in my life with whom everything, or almost everything, was an open book.

By the game's conclusion, James has come to remember the deep resentment he felt in taking care of his wife, Mary, while she was terminally ill, as well as the fact that he killed her before nature could take its course. Much in the way a psychotherapy patient reconnects with a dissociated experience, the unearthing of James's past highlights how profoundly it has continued to influence his present: the faceless monsters echo the way James took Mary's life, blotting out her pale face with a pillow; his half-hearted attempts to serve as savior to Angela reverberate as acts of displaced guilt. But *Silent Hill 2* does not offer a single perspective on how James, or the player, might reconcile the miserable parts of himself and his past with the hope for a better future. Instead— and it's one of the game's most unusual features—you experience your own ending of the game depending on small, often incidental actions taken while playing. These are extrapolated to draw some judgment of the attitudes and proclivities of the player.

The easiest ending to reach, requiring no unusual behavior, is known as the "Leave" ending. James is forgiven by Mary and his murderous act is reframed as a mercy killing; he is permitted to leave the town unscathed. While many games demand the player exert the most effort to attain the morally best ending, *Silent Hill 2* subverts this expectation by offering it freely. The implication is that the player who arrives at Leave has taken the path of least resistance, playing the game in its most obvious form without thinking too much about what it all means. As a reward, he is fed a trite, happy ending, as though the game itself is disdainful of his refusal to take a more idiosyncratic approach to play.

The "Maria" ending unlocks when the player pays special attention to a woman James encounters at various points during the game who looks identical to Mary but behaves in a more provocative, sexualized manner. If the player refuses to look at any mementos of Mary and instead takes pains to protect and look after Maria, the player reaches an ending in which James dismisses his wife as unnecessary baggage and chooses to leave town with her doppelgänger. The player who behaves in this way is drawn to the two-dimensional fantasy that Maria represents, demonstrating a clear preference for her over the complexity of James's relationship with Mary. As James and Maria head to the car in which they'll drive off to what is presumably their new life together, Maria coughs several times, suggesting that she is in the process of contracting the same illness that afflicted Mary. The player has surrendered to impulse and learned nothing from the nightmare of Silent Hill, so there will be no "new" life; the cycle is doomed to repeat itself.

A third ending, "Rebirth," can only be seen if the player has already completed the game at least once. The player must seek out four items scattered throughout the town (which cannot be found on a first play-through) and complete the game with them in hand. The placement of these items is essentially arbitrary and no indication is given as to their purpose or how many are needed to affect an outcome. This player, the game assumes, is obsessed, returning to a hellish place for a second, third, or fourth time, exploring every dark corner despite the terrors that lurk there. The ending, then, is one of feverish, delusional thinking: James takes the four talismans and Mary's body out onto Silent Hill's lake in an attempt to revive her through some mad ritual. Its success or failure is not shown, nor is it necessary, as the point is clear: James is truly lost.

There is another ending to *Silent Hill 2*. It's known as "In Water" and requires, among other things, that James spend much of the game running around at low health, vulnerable to the slightest attack. I never saw that ending. No matter how familiar I became with the game's deformed monsters and unlit hallways, I always found it too nerve-wracking to wander around with my status screen flickering with static and my controller vibrating like a frantic heartbeat: the telltale signs that James was close to death. Instead, I immediately imbibed health potions as soon as I sustained even the slightest injury. The atmosphere of the game was relentlessly disturbing but I was never actually afraid of death because I never let it get close to me. In Water became my white whale: Every time I began a new game, I told myself that this time I'd go for it, and yet every time I fell back on old patterns and received one of the other endings I had seen several times before. Enacting the variables needed for Maria, Rebirth, and even an absurd joke ending called Dog felt effortless to me, yet the road to In Water was impassable, like one of Silent Hill's foggy streets that, defying the laws of physics, terminates at a bottomless pit.

Notably, I had no compunction about reading the details of In Water online. I knew what that ending consisted of, but I avoided experiencing it for myself. I knew that the ending I could not allow myself to see was the one in which James kills himself.

What kind of player got to see In Water? One who was cavalier, reckless. Most of all, the player who was comfortable existing close to death was one who recognized the inconsequential nature of playing a videogame. No actual harm could come to him—he was not James and James was not real, so compassion or care for this avatar's well-being was unnecessary. The game would respond in kind, projecting the player's indifference to digital life onto James who, over a black screen, could be heard to start up his car and peel off at high speed into Silent Hill's lake. "Now I understand the real reason I came to this town," he'd say. "I wonder, what was I afraid of?"[10]

I, unlike this manifestation of James, was afraid of death. More than that, it felt as though the very fabric of time and space had been ruptured by the trauma of Bjorn's suicide. It was the point from which all present problems originated, the marker that distinguished my happy childhood from what I assumed would be the rest of my miserable life. I was unconsciously invested in this idea and sought to reaffirm it in my repeated visits to Silent Hill. By methodically avoiding any risk of in-game death, the suicidal ending of In Water took on a kind of mystique; it was unachievable, unknowable. Despite what I told myself at the start of each play-through, a part of me did not want to see In Water. The superficiality of Leave, the immaturity of Maria, the magical thinking of Rebirth—none of these threatened my sense of self or the world. Happiness *did* seem only skin-deep to me; objectified sexuality *did* resonate as a valid if temporary escape. And though I never believed that I or anyone had the power to bring Bjorn back, I did sometimes fantasize that this was all a spectacular practical joke and one day he would return to school with a smile and a wink, and the pain of the past two years would be erased.

What I refused to tolerate was the idea that a suicidal ending could be "unlocked," that there was a straightforward, prescribed path to it. I could not see In Water because I could not accept that seeing it was so easy. *If it were so obvious, shouldn't I have noticed?* So, I made the ending impossible, spooked myself out of it, convinced myself that in-game death was serious enough to avoid. Any other approach would make In Water and, by extension, my friend's death, mundane—not the unique and magical cause of all my misery. Just a thing that happened.

My relationship with *Silent Hill 2* reflected who I was and what I was going through, not only because of what I played but how I played it. Through this lens, Angela's prophecy of "only the one road" takes on new meaning. The game itself was designed to accommodate multiple paths; it was I, the player, bound by my own psychology, who self-imposed which roads were open and which blocked off. Yet I didn't make these connections at the time, because I didn't know how to talk about games. I'd conditioned myself to *not* talk about them.

It may seem strange that this extended even to my most sacred of spaces, the therapy relationship that had quickly come to represent a sanctuary unlike any other—one matched only, perhaps, by those virtual sanctuaries found throughout my childhood and adolescence in the absolute privacy of game space. But if you were to have asked me why I never mentioned *Silent Hill 2* to Lovett, my guess is that I would have looked at you funny. The idea that my relationship with games might say anything important about me, or anyone, had never crossed my mind.

*

BACK IN THE STAFF MEETING, colleagues and supervisors stared at me, puzzled, hoping to move on to the many other cases on the day's docket. As visions of my life in games and in therapy cycled across my mind's eye like a feverish slide show, I realized that I was reaching back for the one memory that wasn't there, an alternate history in which I gave words to a part of my life that had existed in shadow for decades. There was no recollection to call upon of the time I explained to my father that, yes, in fact, it mattered that the apes escaped. No lightbulb going off to remind me of the session where I told Lovett all about *Silent Hill 2* and my particular way of engaging with it.

I'd only stopped seeing Lovett a year earlier, after a dozen years of productive work. Our therapy helped guide me from a turbulent adolescence to a more stable and optimistic adulthood, and the significance of my chosen career path was not lost on either of us. If this kind of progress was possible without ever talking about games, I thought (as various members of the clinic staff began to look away from me), maybe it wasn't that important after all.

"Sounds like a good fit for Carlos," someone suggested, referring to the "gamer kid."

Carlos was the clinic's substance-abuse specialist. He was late fifties, childless—I doubted he'd played a videogame in his life. I could see where this road led: A treatment focused on excising the abhorrent substance of games, striving toward abstinence so that this young man might live a healthy, game-free life. A shudder ran down my spine. Where would I be without Lovett, true . . . but where would I be without games? At this moment, in this meeting, I couldn't say for sure.

Here's what I could say: The other clinicians in the room thought videogames were simple, but I knew the relationship between a player and a game is complex. They were lumping all games into a monolithic category of "other," but I knew there are many reasons to spend most of one's day inside a digital world. Above all, I knew how important games must be to this young man, whom no one seemed to understand. Like James and Angela on the staircase, he needed someone beside him to acknowledge that his vision of reality was valid and meaningful—even if that vision was of a world on fire.

"I could see him," I said. "I've got space."

Chapter 2

Tutorial

What are videogames?

Learning is the only thing for you. Look what a lot of things there are to learn.

—T. H. White, *The Once and Future King*

SAY YOUR FAVORITE BOOK is *The Once and Future King* by T. H. White (good choice!). Its humor and humanity forever altered the way you think about the power of old stories to inform contemporary problems. Perhaps you first read the novel during a difficult time in your life and its worn pages still bring you comfort in times of need.

Now imagine trying to explain your relationship with *The Once and Future King* to a person who has never read a book before, indeed has made a point of avoiding even reading *about* books. He's heard they can be addictive, and are meant only for children, and then mumbles something about being pretty sure that scientists identified books as a cause of adolescent delinquency. His singular point of contact, he tells you, occurred two years ago when he briefly leafed through a copy of something called *Web Design for Dummies* after a coworker, whom everyone knew to be a bit of a weirdo, left it lying around. He says he found the text indecipherable and felt vindicated in his decision to avoid the medium altogether.

You can picture the skepticism on his face when you say that White's Arthurian epic changed your life. Abandon hope of any nuanced discussion surrounding theme, prose style, or why the work speaks to your lived experience—this person lacks the basic context with which to understand what a book has the potential to be. He is shocked to learn, for instance, that *The Once and Future King* is structured as a narrative, having assumed every book, like the one he scorned a couple of years back, to be a compilation of how-to bullet points. The idea that a book can center around people, places, and events that do not exist in the real world, or that their authors often have creative aspirations beyond instructing readers on how to build a homepage, equally astonishes.

This is how it can feel to try to talk about videogames with those who have little experience with them—it's how I felt coming out of the "gamer kid" staff meeting. There is a fundamental semantic gap, a dearth of shared vocabulary, between those-who-play and those-who-don't. If one's only frames of reference are mainstay work distractors like *Tetris* or *Minesweeper* and I launch into an explanation of *Silent Hill 2*'s grotesque surrealism, I might as well be speaking in tongues.

Lack of exposure is only part of the problem, though, as that lack is rarely coincidental. Like our book-poor friend above, many people deliberately avoid games due to an omnipresent stigma that has spread in mainstream discourse for decades. Games are considered to be fringe, unhealthy, dangerous. Since the late 1990s they have been at the center of fiery political debates about the causes of mass violence—and despite a consistent lack of evidence to support such a connection, public perception has been undeniably impacted. At best games are seen to have the power to frivolously distract, at worst to corrupt and disfigure.

Games are difficult to explain to others because so much of their meaning exists within the bubble of time and space shared only between player and game. Stripped of this context, the game can seem inscrutable. To wit, perhaps the best-known franchise in the medium's history centers around an Italian plumber striving to rescue a princess from turtle monsters with the aid of magic mushrooms. From this vantage point the idea that Mario (first seen in 1981's *Donkey Kong* and appearing since in over two hundred titles) has persisted as a cultural icon for nearly four decades can only strike one as being absurd.

As I began to consider, following the infamous staff meeting, how to think about games from the perspective of a clinical psychologist who assumes meaning behind the thoughts, feelings, and behaviors of others, however trivial they may appear at first glance, I realized that my profession has a similar stigma for people unfamiliar with it. Therapy, too, can appear bafflingly opaque when viewed from outside the patient-therapist relationship. When asked what happens in session, a patient tells her friend, accurately: "We talk." The friend looks at her like she's being taken for a ride. How can "talking" make any appreciable difference in her life?

Our culture is quick to dismiss the psychological as being less real than other domains of life: A medical illness is "serious" while anxiety is "just in your head." If I were to tell a stranger at a party that I'm a dermatologist, this person I've never met before might promptly roll up his sleeve and ask, if it's not too much trouble, that I help put his mind to rest about a mole. But instead I say "clinical psychologist" and the stranger often goes quiet, changes the subject, or awkwardly declares that he'd "better watch" what he says around me. As though merely

speaking to someone fluent in psychological issues would expose him, infect him, in the same way that talking about games
would invite some antisocial or addictive menace to cross his
threshold.

Games and psychotherapy are not innately dangerous, but
their meaning can be hard to grasp from the outside. Their functions, trappings, and potential benefits are inextricably linked
with the relationships in which they occur, whether player-game
or patient-therapist. It is only through looking at these relationships that we might reach a new understanding and the ability
to communicate about games across groups and individuals who
have varying levels of hands-on knowledge.

Any experienced player is familiar with the concept of a "tutorial level" that answers basic questions about how the game
works, ensuring that everyone begins with the same base of information. Here are the questions to be answered in our tutorial:
What is a videogame, exactly? What are the component parts
that make it different from (or similar to) other art forms that
bear far less stigma?

To begin, a working definition: A videogame is an interactive
artwork with a system experienced through a digital interface
such as a computer, television, or phone.

Concise! But let's expand it to incorporate the player-game
relationship: Engaging with a videogame is called play, which
occurs when at least one person (the player) interacts with the
game in time and space, usually through a character who exists
in a setting.

These two sentences, enigmatic though they may seem, are the
beginnings of a bridge. They read as jargon now—the exact kind
of obtuse language that can make games seem so inaccessible to

the uninitiated—but breaking them down will reveal the building blocks from which a game is made.

ALL GAMES HAVE A *SYSTEM:* THE specific mechanics that dictate the rules of the game and how the player interacts with it. System is the most distinguishing feature that separates games from other forms of play. When two children participate in a spirited bout of cops and robbers, their action is limited only by imagination. The "cop" fires his gun, only for the "robber" to announce that she is protected by a bulletproof forcefield, which the cop counters by declaring that he is, in fact, an alien from outer space whose weaponry bypasses all forcefield technology. As long as everyone involved agrees to the shared fantasy of what is taking place, the play continues.*

In games, action is restricted by both the player's imagination and what the game allows. While this is not uniquely true of videogames (the rules of *Monopoly* do not allow players to plan a daring prison escape should they wind up incarcerated), the boundary of system is firmest within virtual worlds. Games played in physical space—such as board games, tabletop role-playing games, and sports—are arbitrated by human beings. Rules can be negotiated, modified, or thrown out entirely. Videogame players ultimately answer to the computer, and so they cannot attempt anything that has not been programmed.

In *Tetris,* for example, which has existed in countless forms since its introduction in 1984, the governing rule is simple: Blocks of various shapes fall from the top of the screen to the bottom and the player must arrange them to form rows with-

---

* We will return to the similarities and crucial differences between this kind of unstructured play and the act of playing a videogame in Chapter 4.

out any gaps. Each filled row or rows disappear and make room for more rows. The system can be further elaborated in terms of how the game progresses (each block falls at a slightly faster rate than the last), how it ends (the screen grows so cluttered that no more blocks can fall), how it's scored (players earn points for rows cleared; the more rows cleared at a time, the higher the point value), the role of chance (the shape of a given falling block is arbitrarily determined), and, crucially, the player's options for interaction (as a block falls, the player may move it left or right, rotate it, or accelerate its descent).

As most games severely limit what actions are possible at any given moment, emphasis tends to fall on mastery over freedom. The limited options in *Tetris*—left, right, down, or rotate—pale by an order of magnitude in comparison to the near-infinite possibilities available to children playing pretend or to a group of friends playing a more structured (but still human-run) role-playing game like *Dungeons & Dragons*. As a result, the player's focus is likely to center on getting better at *Tetris*'s relatively simple mechanics rather than more open-ended experimentation, as there are not many components with which to experiment.

As systems grow more complex, the opportunity for experimentation grows, too, though still within the boundaries of what the game is designed to accommodate. Even the story-based titles that absorbed so much of my youth—which demanded few of the fine-motor skills required of a game like *Tetris* while emphasizing slow-paced exploration and lateral thinking—feature restrictive systems. Options are more abundant than in *Tetris,* but the player can still only interact with certain objects in the game world and those objects can only be used in ways the game has anticipated. When the player arrives at a closed cottage door in

The Black Cauldron, the only productive action is likely for him to press the "interact" key, at which point the game will decide whether this means the player's character opens the door or is informed that it's locked. The player cannot kick the door down, peer through a keyhole, or make meowing sounds to try to confuse the people within—the game is not programmed to deal with any of these eventualities. However rich and detailed the world, the player must ultimately learn the system that governs it in order to understand to what extent he is able to interact with the game.

By imposing strict limits on what is possible and giving direction in terms of what one should do in order to master the game, one could argue that system's overarching effect is to provide the player with the game's "point": the purpose for playing. In the original version of *Tetris,* the directive is to earn the highest score possible, achieved through a combination of how long the player can go before her screen is filled and how effective she is in clearing multiple rows at a time. *The Black Cauldron* compels the player to guide its story in order to find out what happens to its cast of characters. Often these baked-in goals are sufficient; they structure and define her experience of the game. But if you'll recall my father's searching query—"What's the point?"—the meaning behind play can be more nebulous than what the game itself dictates. Like so much else, meaning is ultimately forged in the relationship between player and game. Purpose is the singular freedom that no game, no matter how limiting its system, can entirely restrain.

In the early 1990s my brother and I competed for high scores on numerous games we shared on our handheld Nintendo Game Boy, including *Tetris.* But when the excitement of seeing one set of our initials above the other's on the in-game leaderboard wore thin, we began to devise new ways to vie for supremacy. "Pure *Tetris*" was one of my brother's most devilish concoctions, in which the player had to clear four rows at a time, the maximum number possible and the most difficult configuration to consistently achieve. Of course, the ones and zeros within our little grey *Tetris* cartridge knew nothing of this bastardization of its system: Should I accidentally clear a single row it would continue dropping the next block as normal. But my brother, watching vigilantly over my shoulder, would pluck the Game Boy out of my hand, flick the on-off switch to restart it, and begin his own attempt—imposing our system over the game's.

Player-derived systems are commonplace. They can be a means to increase difficulty or spice up competition, as in our "pure *Tetris*" variant, to justify returning to a game the player has already mastered or even to test the limits of the game's innate system. Speed-runs are a popular way of pursuing one or all three of these goals: as evident in their name, they represent a player's attempt to complete a game from start to finish as quickly as possible. This often requires not only intimate familiarity with the game—one's ability to even attempt a speed-run is proof of mastery—but also the employment of creative methods to bend or break the game's seemingly inviolate rules, either through exploiting software glitches or engaging the system in ways that the game clearly did not intend.

As of July 2019 the world record speed-run for the action-adventure title *The Legend of Zelda: Ocarina of Time,* a game that could easily take a first-time player thirty hours to complete, stood at a little under seventeen minutes.[11] The player who accomplished this feat not only took advantage of certain hard-to-find errors in the game's code that allowed him to skip large portions of the game but also spent as much of his run as possible moving in reverse. For reasons that even Nintendo, the game's developer, likely could not satisfactorily explain, the player's avatar in *Ocarina of Time* moves slightly faster when running backward. Watching the video of the record-setting run is thus a paradoxical affair in which the player acts with the utmost precision and knowledge, while his proxy on screen seems to happily stumble into all the right places without bothering to look where he's going.

The game a speed-runner plays is fundamentally different from the one played by someone "as intended," yet both represent an effort to derive purpose from finite possibility. Whether one invests herself in the story, combat, and puzzle-solving of *Ocarina of Time,* or enjoys exploiting its idiosyncrasies in the self-appointed interest of speed, the player engages with a rules-bound virtual world in a way that makes sense to her, that offers her some kind of meaning.

PATRICIA, A PATIENT I SAW for weekly psychotherapy for a number of years, once recounted to me her singular requirement when shopping for a new game: It had to be big. The lush wetlands of a fantasy kingdom or the streets of a crime-ridden city were immaterial as compared to sheer size. Not surprisingly, she was drawn to "open world" games, so-called because of the immensity of their virtual environments and their emphasis on the player's freedom to do or not do as she pleases within them. Typically, there is a central storyline that the player may follow, but tasks associated with this route pale in comparison to the myriad locations, interactions, and challenges that the player can discover through self-guided exploration. The system in these titles is defined by the designers' efforts to disguise that there is a system. This is never truly possible, of course, but the illusion of an unfettered world can be facilitated by highlighting breadth over depth. By leaning into the strength of a computer-powered medium, the most successful open-world games are so chock full of stuff to do and places to go that the limitations of how deeply the player can engage with any specific instance feels less overbearing and engenders the liberating sensation that she can go anywhere or do anything.

For Patricia, living in a massive game world was the primary purpose of playing. She rarely played more than one game at a time, preferring instead to mine a single title until she felt she had exhausted everything it had to offer. A virtual world so large and dense that many players will only see a fraction of everything within it can be intimidating to some, particularly those who derive satisfaction from feeling that they have unambiguously completed a game. But Patricia said she depended on games not running out of material. "I don't see the point of starting if I know it will be over in a few hours," she told me.

When we began working together, "her game," as she often referred to it, was *Fallout 4*, released in 2015 and set in postapocalyptic New England. Considered to be on the smaller end of contemporary open-world standards in terms of geographic area, one estimate placed the game's map at about one square mile of virtual terrain—it would take a player's character eleven minutes to sprint across it from end to end.[12] There is no particular reason to do so, however, as that square mile is densely packed with characters to interact with and missions to complete, as well as the more open-ended tasks of scrounging for weapon and armor modifications, and building settlements in the irradiated deserts of post-nuclear Massachusetts.

At a moderate clip, forsaking many of the optional paths and details the world has to offer, *Fallout*'s central plot can be completed in well under sixty hours. Patricia logged over six hundred. She wasn't bad at the game—far from it. She played *Fallout* in "survival mode," a setting that modified the game's system to more realistically simulate the brutality and challenge of post-apocalyptic existence. In this mode, the player's character had to eat, drink, and sleep regularly, with numerous caveats to these necessities. Sleeping less than seven in-game hours at a stretch yielded limited benefit; the unsanitary overuse of a single mattress could lead to illness; food had to be consumed regularly, but if the player's character ever resorted to cannibalism to fulfill this requirement, no other food source would satisfy her moving forward. "Fast travel," a feature that allowed the player to instantly teleport to locations she had previously visited, was disabled in this mode. The basic act of navigating the game world was a slow, considered process.

In brief, survival mode made *Fallout* much, much harder and surely from some players' points of view it renders the game an unplayable slog. But Patricia relished the opportunity to live more authentically inside the game, which felt even bigger for all the extra work survival mode demanded from her to move about and stay alive. Patricia deliberately avoided *Fallout*'s main storyline and the basic concerns of food, water, and shelter provided endless justification to eschew completing the game in favor of prolonging her time in its world.

TIME IS ANOTHER IMPORTANT COMPONENT of games, and one that can be difficult to define. At its most concrete, it is measured in the number of hours the player spends with a given title—for a player like Patricia that number can climb striking-ly high, particularly for someone unfamiliar with the medium. What could she possibly be doing in there for so many hours? A social worker by training, Patricia mostly did not binge on *Fallout*—her job as a claims supervisor for a local insurance company, as well as obligations caring for her ill mother, ab-sorbed too much of a given day to allow for extended play ses-sions. Rather, she would return to the game methodically during free moments—one or two hours here or there on evenings and weekends—slowly accruing her impressive time over the course of nearly a year.

Virtual time is a beast of a different nature. Often the player's actions in physical time will roughly match time in the game—the fraction of a second it takes to press a controller button is about equal to the fraction of a second it takes for the player's character to swing a sword, say, or open a car door. In other instances, a few moments of play may represent the passage of hours, years or decades in the game world, as the player settles cities, builds armies or wages war.

Regardless of scope, the game invariably exercises its freedom to bend or break the laws of physical time. Many patients, includ-ing Patricia, have talked to me about the fantasy of time travel—not in the H. G. Wells sense of visiting eons past and future, but the more personal desire to return to an earlier time in one's life and "replay" it with all the wisdom accrued in the intervening years. Patricia would sometimes ruminate over romantic and aca-demic paths not taken, wishing she could go back to being twelve years old, or twenty, or an event from last week and try again with her present mind intact. Here was the instinctive human pull toward mastery, the idea that through repetition of the same situation—in which the only changing variable was the individual's own knowledge and skills—the traumas of the past could be avoided and thus undone. Games often indulge this fantasy: Whenever the player's character dies and is reset to some earlier point in the game, this represents a bold affront to the notion of time as a straight line. The player retains an awareness of what's to come that her on-screen character could not logically know, benefitting through interaction with the real world, where time moves only forward.

In the interests of making the experience more streamlined and enjoyable for the player, the manipulation of time in games extends far beyond the undoing of death or other failures. *Fallout*'s open world progresses through day-night cycles about every seventy-two minutes instead of every twenty-four hours. Savvy players can even hack the game and alter this variable, making game-time more or less in sync with real-time. Patricia would do this frequently, slowing down the pace of the virtual world to make the most out of the hour or two she had set aside to play, as certain activities in the game could only occur during in-game daylight hours. *Fallout* also distinguished how time passes depending on what's happening: mostly it moves forward independent of the player's actions, but when engaged in combat the player has the ability to freeze time in order to tactically select how she would like to target her enemies.

The coming together of physical and virtual time can be engrossing or disorienting for the player. The speed with which the game world moves forward—and the efficiency with which complex goals can be accomplished—can lead to the subjective experience of real-world time flashing by in an instant: The player turns off the game to realize six hours have passed. Whether this realization is problematic or pleasant depends on the player and her relationship with the game. Had she intended to spend this much of her day with the game—does it feel like time well spent—or does she feel robbed of something, sucked into a fabricated world only to be spat back out into the real one after the sun has set, or risen?

SPACE IN GAMES ALSO REPRESENTS a melding of the corporeal and virtual, an emergent world-between-worlds that only comes into being through the relationship between player and game. The player lives in physical reality, while the game, unplayed, is trapped as digital information in virtual reality. When the two come together, game-space is formed.

The road between worlds is two-way: Unlike most other forms of media—books, theater, films, and television—the player is not only observer but participant. The game generates thoughts and feelings in the player and the player attempts to exert his influence on the game through behavior, usually by manipulating some physical object that translates into virtual information. A keyboard and mouse, touch-screen, or console controller serves as nexus point between worlds. One of a game's chief attractions is that its translation of limited physical action into a fabricated virtual world allows mundane physical behaviors to feel extraordinary. The subtlest of gestures, such as the click of a mouse, often corresponds to in-game action of far greater significance. This action may represent something that, in the physical world, is beyond what the player is capable of (dunking a basketball), what any single person is capable of (chopping down a forest), or what is fundamentally possible (shooting lightning bolts out of an enchanted staff).

It is undeniable that part of the thrill of time and space in videogames lies in the promise to make the difficult easy, the impossible possible. Shooting a three-pointer in *NBA 2K17* is easier to do than on a basketball court; shredding the solo to Rush's "Tom Sawyer" on *Guitar Hero*'s five-button controller is simpler to pull off than on a six-stringed Les Paul. But the virtual rewards of game-space do not translate literally when the game is shut down: Putting ten thousand hours into *NBA 2K17* will not make you an all-star basketball player (though it will likely make you an exceptional *NBA 2K17* player) and mastering *Guitar Hero* will not, despite helping to develop some relevant motor skills, make you a master guitarist.

So why do it? This, at least in part, was the question I set out to answer emerging from the "gamer kid" meeting. In certain games, and for certain players, a principal reward lies in mastery of the game's system (or one's own self-imposed system), as I have suggested. The entirety of a game like *Tetris* can be more or less encapsulated in the ideas of system, time, and space—these are the ingredients needed to understand how the player relates to the game and what meaning she likely derives from it. But many other games require two additional building blocks—character and setting—to adequately elucidate what is happening in game-space that the player finds valuable and worth investing time and energy.

The player's representation within game-space—that is, her *character*—is the vessel through which all the thrills and frustrations of play are vicariously experienced. In some cases, such as in *Fallout,* the player can build her character from the ground up, dictating broad strokes like gender, height, and build, as well as tweaking minute facial details from jawline to nose size to type of earlobe; adding tattoos and scars; perfecting hairstyle, clothing, and accessories. The player is free to sculpt herself from unmolded clay and, in so doing, identify an aspect of herself within its form. Identification—the process of locating oneself in an external subject—is often central to the enduring appeal of game characters and the emotional attachment players develop toward them.

How the player approaches the freedom of character creation in a game like *Fallout* says a great deal about how she relates to her character and thus what aspects of herself she is exploring through the prism of the game. One player might build a character that resembles herself in real life as closely as possible; another builds an idealized proxy, an Adonis of culturally valued traits; still others may gravitate toward a character that, at least on the surface, seems completely unrelated to who she is in the physical world.

Patricia's character was a man, and ugly. She made him short, stocky, with beady eyes and a bulbous nose, short-cropped, neon green hair and unsightly blemishes covering his face. Her initial insights into why she had meticulously crafted this particular avatar were superficial, to say the least. "I thought he looked funny," she told me. But to leave the matter there would be to discard the significant time she spent building her character—not to mention playing as him—as meaningless. From a physical perspective, Patricia was the inverse of her *Fallout* character. Tall, slender, with striking, angular features, she had explored being a fashion model in her late teens in lieu of attending university.

Patricia returned home unannounced one day from an extended stint in Europe, telling her mother that she had changed her mind about her career path and that she wanted to go back to school. It would be years before she disclosed to anyone that she had been sexually assaulted by a photographer after a shoot, beginning a spiral of anxiety and shame. The once glamorous idea of being a model had become repugnant to her.

Over time, Patricia became willing to consider that her *Fallout* character—whom she referred to as "Pat"—was not a random creation. She desired him as an alter-ego precisely because he looked undesirable: Having long internalized her physical attractiveness as the cause of unwanted advances from men, Patricia found solace in playing as a character with a face that, as she put it, "not even a mother could love." This sentiment also belied the resentment Patricia felt in acting as caretaker to her mother, the woman who had pushed Patricia into pageantry and modeling from pre-adolescence. Pat was a repudiation of everything people had told Patricia made her special, yet still he survived, hour after hour, in the unforgiving wastes of *Fallout* (and in survival mode, no less). He symbolized freedom from the expectations of family and society; as no one could possibly want anything from such a creature, Patricia could inhabit him for an hour here or there in order to take care of herself.

Not all games grant the wide latitude of *Fallout* to build one's character from the ground up. Often a game's character is a predetermined individual whose goals, interests, sense of humor and so on, may or may not be aligned with the player's. Settling into this relationship demands a different kind of identification: Rather than creating a character based on who the player wants to be within the game, the player must find a way to connect with the pathos of an extant personality. Wish-fulfillment is a common point of entry, as characters frequently represent qualities that the player venerates in fantasy but struggles to manifest in real life. A character who is cool, confident, and endowed with superhuman abilities intoxicates a player who feels powerless or unappreciated outside of the game—or who simply thinks it would be exciting to be a ninja, a marine, or Batman.

But the desire to embody a more powerful version of oneself is only one way in which players may relate to a preset character. The enduring appeal of Mario—the short, cartoonish plumber who's good at jumping and not much else—since his introduction in 1981 cannot plausibly be explained by his manifesting the apex of coolness or power. For many, this unlikely hero instead stands as a paragon of stability and timelessness, a comforting acknowledgement that, even as we age, we do not transform into completely different people. In response to the question, "Why do people like Mario?" placed on an internet message board, one poster responded, "He's a character we grew up with . . . and he hasn't changed one bit."[13]

Preset characters cannot be customized and fine-tuned by players, and that means incompatibilities invariably arise within the relationship. In the most extreme cases a player may feel so psychologically distant from her in-game proxy that she abandons the game or plays through with a rote detachment. In other instances, however, the player may ultimately embrace the vicarious adoption of an unfamiliar or atypical role, which can in turn lead to new emotional experience.

Hellblade: Senua's Sacrifice, released in 2017, was designed with the unusual goal of realistically depicting the psychotic experience of its main character. Senua is a Pict warrior traumatized by the loss of her beloved; she spends the game navigating Norse-inspired dreamscapes while fighting off merciless skeletal warriors and trying to cope with the incessant voices in her head. Events that can lead to Senua's death are often set off without any clear indication of what the player is supposed to do to survive and the game makes the claim early on that if Senua dies too many times (though what constitutes "too many" is not specified), she will not be resurrected, and the player's saved game file will be deleted.

One reviewer, Nathan Grayson for the games website Kotaku, expressed his initial frustration with this brutal approach: It seemed unfair for the game to punish him and Senua for not knowing how to do things before giving him a chance to learn. But as Grayson pressed on, he realized that *Hellblade* was "about a character who's far past the point of learning the basics, or even being at the height of her powers. Senua's on the brink of a total breakdown."[14] By presenting an unconventional character, *Hellblade* invited the player to access parts of himself that elsewhere in life he might prefer to avoid: feelings of confusion, helplessness, and dread. "I'm anxious as hell," Grayson wrote of playing the game. "Every time Senua takes a hit, I wince in real life." He identified with her emotional experience, bonded to it, and through that connection a compelling reason to play emerged.

Despite its intensity and bleakness, Grayson concluded his review: "I'm dreading the prospect of playing, but . . . I've decided despite my fears and anxieties—to press on."

The player's relationship with his character is not always defined by identification. Sometimes the bond is closer to objectification, the empathy implicit in putting oneself in the character's shoes replaced by the catharsis derived from exerting one's will on another without resistance.

"It wasn't really about trying to get people to imagine they *were* Lara Croft," *Tomb Raider* creator Toby Gard admitted during the same interview in which he marveled, with a hint of contrition, over players' obsessions with murdering his signature creation. "My understanding was that . . . games, particularly at that time, were played by guys. . . . There was a strange power thing that people were experiencing over this virtual character."[15] That "strange power thing" is not always sadistic in nature: Gard pointed out that players often seemed to oscillate between regarding themselves as Croft's guardian angel and being her cruel puppet master.

Which role the player inhabits—protector or torturer—speaks directly to how he is relating to the game and his character within it at that specific moment in time. Take, for example, a scene from an episode of the UK comedy series *Spaced*.[16] Twenty-something man-child Tim Bisley, one of the show's lead characters, is gloomily playing a videogame when his eccentric neighbor, Brian, walks into the apartment.

"What are you playing?" Brian asks.

"*Tomb Raider 3*," Tim replies.

The television (on which we also see the reflection of Tim's disaffected face) shows Croft swimming through a submerged cavern. Suddenly, she begins to convulse and choke.

"She's drowning," Brian observes, mournful yet transfixed.

"Yeah."

Lara releases a final gasp and her thrashing ceases; she hangs lifeless in the water.

"Is that the point of the game?" Brian asks.

Tim shrugs. "It depends what mood you're in, really."

Tim feels depressed in the first place because he has just received a vapid letter from his ex-girlfriend attempting to explain why she dumped him. He has turned to Croft to nurse this wound, finding solace in unfettered control over a woman literally designed to stoke male heterosexual fantasy. In acknowledging that his murderous in-game behavior is dependent on mood, Tim points toward the complex dynamic he has formed with this character, one with the power to move from altruism to sadism, love to hate. Tim chooses to drown Lara *because* he loves her, as he loved his ex. By killing her, knowing she will resurrect, he participates in a kind of mourning ritual. The last shot of the scene shows Lara, alive and well, jumping back into the water at Tim's direction. He is trying to undo his pain, make right in the virtual world something that feels irreparably wrong in his actual life.*

Whether built from scratch or preset and grounded in identification or objectification, the characters outlined so far are analogous in a fundamental way: Each represents a single individual living within a larger world for the player to inhabit. In some games, however, the player's role cannot be situated within any tangible avatar—instead, she plays as formless decision-maker. These are often called "god games," in which players may be responsible for running a city over the course of in-game years, a society over the course of in-game centuries, or squadrons of soldiers in relative real-time. The player still fulfills a role within the game world (mayor, dictator or military commander, respectively) and may be addressed as such by other characters in the game, but she is privileged to a level of omniscience and precision that far exceeds the capabilities of any real individual.

In these cases, the player's relationship with character is less about identification or objectification toward an in-game counterpart as it is about interpersonal connection with all the other

---

* The limits of this approach to mourning will be addressed in Chapter 9.

characters in the game (non-player characters, often abbreviated as NPCs).* Whereas we have looked to the player's character as a means of understanding how the player might represent and experiment with different aspects of himself in virtual time and space, NPCs can help us understand how the player relates to others and copes with social problems such as conflict and loss.

XCOM: Enemy Unknown, released in 2012, is a tactics and strategy game in which the player inhabits the unseen Commander, charged with guiding small groups of soldiers on international missions to thwart alien invaders. In the mode of *Fallout* and others, the player can manipulate the appearance and characteristics of his squad members, from gender to physical features to nationality. But *XCOM*'s stroke of subtle brilliance was that it also allowed the player to name those men and women whom he would be placing in harm's way.

A friend of mine, David, once described a relationship with *XCOM* that was not inconsistent with how I heard the game discussed elsewhere, both online and with other friends. He appreciated the opportunity to customize his ragtag military outfit and, rather than inventing names out of thin air, David felt naturally inclined to assign each of his soldiers the moniker of someone he knew in real life. He delighted in telling me—and I felt some measure of pride in hearing—that the NPC who bore my name was one of his go-to snipers who had survived many hard-won skirmishes. Animating characters with names from real life made the victories of these characters more meaningful: singular

---

* Relationships with NPCs are often a vital aspect of games in which the player has a tangible character. But for illustration's sake, "god games" are particularly demonstrative of the emotional power of computer-controlled others as, lacking a visible avatar, the player has nowhere else to project his psychology.

achievements by a known person rather than an interchangeable array of procedurally generated 3-D models. But with affinity and personal connection came the possibility of a more challenging emotional experience. David described to me a situation in which one of his soldiers, whom he called Marcello after another friend, was killed on the battlefield. David felt entirely unwilling to accept this loss—to bury a character who represented a unique amalgam of the real and virtual—whom he loved in life outside the game and, through that affection, had come to feel a modicum of love for inside the game.

David tried his best to take advantage of the malleable time and space endemic to *XCOM*. He loaded the save, only to have Marcello die again. He tried it every possible way, studying the scenario and the consequences of choosing one route over another. And every time it ended the same way: the soldier was surrounded, pinned down, and killed. Marcello had to die, and David had to accept it. Doing so was not traumatic in the way loss in the physical world can be; David knew implicitly that game-space could not reach outside the boundaries of *XCOM*. Yet even though the death of "Marcello" went away when the game was turned off, the experience of letting go stayed with David, becoming a point of reflection in terms of what the game had meant to him.

LASTLY, WE COME TO *SETTING:* whether a medieval kingdom, an abandoned spaceship, or 1940s France, nearly all games have one. Setting provides the context for the player's character and actions within the game world. It is the aspect of games that most overlaps with other media, and interest in a particular genre of film or literature may draw a player to games that share a familiar setting. Someone like Patricia was as happy to dive into fantasy as she was into science fiction, as long as her other requirements for the title were met, but others will gravitate toward a game that features a resonant setting. For instance, a colleague once mentioned to me that he had purchased the *Lord of the Rings*–branded action title *Middle-earth: Shadow of War* despite middling reviews because he would "play, read, or watch anything" set in Tolkien's universe.

Games permit a deeper immersion into setting than other media, as the player can explore and affect the world at his direction in a way that is not possible when reading a book or watching a movie. This means a player's relationship with a game's setting may go beyond its content per se and extend to how that content can be explored. Recall the unexpected commercial success of the meditative puzzle game *Myst:* the public's fascination with it, as well as my own, was not rooted in the popularity of the wandering-around-a-quiet-island genre of movies or books, if such a genre even existed. But *Myst*'s appeal *was* rooted in a human pastime that predated games, movies, and perhaps even the written word—walking around quiet, beautiful places—and the novelty of enjoying that experience in a virtual space rather than a park or garden in the physical world. Contemporary so-called "walking simulators" like 2015's *Everybody's Gone to the Rapture* continue in this tradition: While that title's setting (a small village in the English countryside) may not come across as enticing on paper, its meticulously realized detail and the player's ability to dig as finely into its minutiae as she likes brings meaning into the experience that would be lost in another medium.

Now let's return to our definition: A videogame is an interactive artwork with a system experienced through a digital interface. Engaging with a videogame is called play, which occurs when at least one person (the player) interacts with the game in time and space, usually through a character who exists in a setting.

With these foundational concepts demystified—a common language established—we can move forward with a deeper exploration of where games (and the stigma surrounding them) come from, why we play them, when they help and when they hurt, and how to talk about games and players in ways both critical and compassionate.

Chapter 3

Uploaded Unconscious

Where did videogames come from?

When guilty shame wears a mask of curiosity,
men are turned inside out, becoming strangers
to themselves.

—Kobo Abe, *Secret Rendezvous*

ON JUNE 7, 1954, Alan Turing ate an apple laced with cyanide. For the previous two years the pioneering mathematician—whose foundational work in computer science played a direct role in the Allied victory of World War II—lived as a pariah, shunned by colleagues and chemically castrated under orders of the UK government. This ignominious decline was catalyzed by Turing's conviction in 1952 for the crime of homosexuality, the same year that he arguably created the world's first videogame.[17]

If we adhere strictly to the definition laid out in the last chapter, Turing's famous chess program doesn't quite qualify. There was no "digital interface" on which the game could be played because no computer in existence was powerful enough to run Turing's code. At the very least, though, his was one of the first theoretical videogames, which Turing approximated by recruiting a colleague to act as the human player while Turing himself made moves based solely on the algorithm he had written.

Turing (or, more accurately, his program) lost the match, but then that wasn't really the point. His interest resided in the broader goal of a computerized "brain" that might be capable of learning and mastering a game like chess over time: in other words, the creation of artificial intelligence. Turing's dream of meaningful interaction with a digital world cannot be disentangled from his lifetime spent repressing a sexuality seen as vile and illicit by contemporary society.

One of the most enduring contributions of Sigmund Freud's psychoanalysis, which by the mid-twentieth century was on its way to becoming a mainstream ideology in the US and UK, was its dismantling of the notion of coincidence. By centering its theories on the unconscious—the portion of mental life that exists beneath awareness yet exerts influence on our behavior— psychoanalysis proffered the unpleasant but enduring truth that, to paraphrase Freud, "We are not masters in our own house."[18] Anxieties, fantasies, and conflicts that feel too threatening to be consciously appraised nevertheless worm through our minds and bodies to resolve themselves by whatever means available. The unconscious is filled with taboo desires because the unconscious knows nothing of societal norms: Sexuality and aggression are its primary energies and, like rushing rivers, these energies carve out channels according to the contours of tolerability for the individual and the broader culture in which that person lives—but they have to go somewhere.

The neo-Freudians of Turing's day, in their incessant efforts to catalogue the psyche's defense mechanisms, might have labeled his fascination with AI as a form of sublimation: the act of redirecting a socially unacceptable impulse (in this case, homosexual desire) into productive, socially valued work (computer science).

In the realities of his world Turing could not have a child or even openly love a partner, but perhaps he could birth a learning computer—which he might presumably have instilled with more progressive values than the prevailing ones of his time.

Interpreting the unconscious can be fraught, as it's hard to disprove motivation that by definition operates beneath the surface. The fall of psychoanalysis as the dominant form of mental health treatment began in the late 1970s and was driven in large part by the fact that psychoanalysis had become a defender of the status quo. Social problems—such as intolerance of homosexuality—could be misconstrued as psychological illness—such as a patient being told his homosexuality signified an unhealthy deviance from "normal" sexual functioning—and a patient refusing this explanation could be dismissed as resistant to the analyst's authority. This kind of tyrannical head-shrinking was never Freud's intention, nor is it the intention of competent psychoanalytic psychotherapists practicing today. At its core, psychoanalysis was designed to oppose, not embody, conservative forces: It was initially and at its best remains a heuristic treatment, one based on the notion that the truth, no matter how disturbing, will ultimately set you free.

Attempting to armchair psychoanalyze a long-dead mathematician holds limited value. Yet my assertion that Turing wrote his chess program in part as a way to cope with his sexual orientation takes on greater validity when it is viewed as the first in a series of similar data points: namely, that the creation, expansion, and stigmatization of videogames is rooted in the experience of shame. Overlooked in histories of videogames, these points reveal a correlation that, due to their repetition across time and space over the course of decades, is hard to deny as real and are no less so for existing outside conscious awareness. Games have at times represented an escape from the judgmental outside world as they did for Turing; in other cases, they have acted as the source of humiliation, real or imagined.

A former supervisor of mine once referred to shame as the most difficult emotion to approach in psychotherapy. The more you name it, she warned, the more powerful it feels to the patient. Directing the patient's attention to disavowed anger or sadness—making the unconscious conscious—can prove cathartic. Doing so allows the patient's feelings to flow down canals that lead to their proper targets: one gets angry about being mistreated or cries over a loss, rather than steering the same energy destructively toward the self. But shame has nowhere else to go: the target is always the self. It is a learned emotion, born when someone makes us feel that who we are is fundamentally wrong or bad, and is reinforced over time. Unlike embarrassment, which is a feeling of discomfort over what others might think, shame is an internalization of that external judgment, and to draw a patient's attention to it often sets the very cycle in motion that the therapist is trying to help him break out of: *Yes, you're right, I am ashamed, my God, how pathetic, why do I care so much what other people think, I'm such a loser. . . .* The way through shame is to challenge the basic premise on which it is founded: an unenviable task for the patient, as he must learn to defy the world as he knows it, whether by dethroning a figure whose authority has never been questioned (such as a parent) or refusing to assimilate a social rule over which he has no direct control (such as a law against homosexuality).

Due to the natural human aversion toward bringing it into consciousness, shame's role in the development of games has been easy to miss—because we actively, if unconsciously, have avoided seeing it. But it's been there, unerring, for three-quarters of a century, persisting to the present day. A 2017 technology buying guide by *The New York Times* columnist Lucas Peterson featured the following line: "I'd also like a Nintendo Switch [games console] . . . which seems like a great way to kill some time on a long train ride or flight. I like videogames—maybe more than I'd care to admit."[19] In 2018 BuzzFeed published a game-centered holiday gift guide by Heather Braga that opened with an animated GIF of a cartoon character, eyes bloodshot and twitching, holding a controller. "Do you live with someone who looks just like this?" Braga began. "*Sigh,* I do."[20] These attitudes are so ubiquitous as to seem hardly worth noting. But if we pause for a moment and draw our attention to these statements, we might wonder: Why should Peterson be ashamed to admit that he likes games or feel compelled to qualify their value as mere time-killers? Why did Braga choose to open her list of recommended gifts for videogame-players on an exasperated, almost apologetic note? Whence comes this unholy marriage of shame and digital play? The answer is, from the beginning.

Following World War II—and thanks in no small part to Turing's innovations—computers represented the next wave of technological development. They were of great interest to governments and academic institutions for their calculating efficiency, not to mention the untapped potential presented by a new branch of applied science. Like Turing and his chess program, others entering the nascent field saw games as a clever way to test and demonstrate the power of their machines: games like chess were, after all, bound by relatively simple rules governing vast complexity, and the public's familiarity with those games would make what the computer was doing behind the scenes appear simultaneously accessible and impressive. But the initial paradox of leveraging cutting-edge scientific equipment to build playful diversions generated a thread of discomfort that has followed games ever since.

Contemporary with Turing's chess match, the British computer company Ferranti developed a machine that could play the simple parlor game Nim.* This was conceived as a media-friendly way to showcase the calculating capacity of Ferranti's computer, dubbed the Nimrod, when it was unveiled at the 1951 Festival of Britain. But the desire to be understood and appreciated by computing neophytes came with a fear of oversimplification: Focusing their mysterious new technology through the prism of a game, the company's scientific achievement might be dismissed as childish novelty. A line from an accompanying instruction manual revealed Ferranti's concern that the Nimrod's jocular function would be misinterpreted: "It may appear that, in trying to make machines play games, we are wasting our time."[21] The guide goes on to insist that a game-playing computer merely exemplifies how the technology could be oriented toward practical (that is, worthwhile) problems, reading like a preemptive defense against the presumed judgment of others.

By the late 1960s and early '70s, the computer industry in the US and Europe had grown far beyond the creation of one-off machines to be exhibited at fairs, but the machines themselves remained a rare commodity. They were the size of a room, for one, and only accessible at the few private companies, govern-

---

* This game of picking up matchsticks features fewer possible combinations of moves than chess by several orders of magnitude. Thus, unlike Turing, Ferranti was able to build a computer powerful enough to actually run its code.

ment agencies, and universities that could afford them. In accordance with these settings, computers were by this time utilized to perform no shortage of practical tasks as conceived by financiers, NASA scientists, and academic researchers alike. Games were no longer needed as a proof of concept; the value of computers was readily apparent to the elite few who might come into contact with them.

By all accounts, then, videogames should have disappeared.* Computers were serious machines for conducting serious business; no one needed to apologize sheepishly for wasting time with them as they had in the days of Ferranti. The idea of mass-market personal computing—which would eventually catalyze the commercial games industry—was still years away; there was no logical place for frivolity within the ivory towers of innovation and research that housed the most sophisticated technological instruments in the world. Nevertheless, certain programmers began of their own accord to leverage the unprecedented computing power at their disposal toward less scholarly ends.

It is worth noting that in the middle of a book arguing for the nuance and complexity of games, I am here about to construct a highly selective history of them—one that at times may seem to paint their architects and proponents as devious and deviant. By following the development of games through the white, middle-class American men who made and played them, I will entirely overlook the myriad contributions to games made over the years by people of diverse genders and ethnicities, not to

---

* Or been relegated, at least, to the coin-op arcades starting to pop up across North America, western Europe, and Japan. These games centers, aimed at relieving children of their weekly allowances, featured devices both mechanical (such as pinball machines) and electric—but the latter were Neolithic as compared with the processing power of computers.

mention the instrumental role of developers and publishers from other nations, particularly Japan and more recently South Korea and various European nations. Instead, this version of history illustrates the development of mainstream games and popular opinion of them to the present day. In the same way that we are influenced by the psychological narratives we tell ourselves about our families and experiences, the purpose here is less objective fact than subjective truth.

Not all games are violent or sexualized; not all players and creators of games are straight white men; not all straight white men who play games are obsessed with violence or sex. Even if not factual, though, these ideas have been regarded as true in the public consciousness for decades. To confront and ultimately revise these narratives it is essential to understand how they came to be. As Turing turned to games as an escape from shame and Ferranti felt some measure of shame for turning to games as a means of self-promotion, following generations would continue to wrestle with the notion of games as cause of and solution to shameful emotions. Games would alternately serve as a perpetuator of and cathartic outlet for this tension, a kind of digital repository for the taboo and countercultural fantasies of a repressed group of mainstream Americans: an uploaded unconscious.

IN 1975 WILL CROWTHER FOUND HIMSELF on the far side of a painful divorce. As a programmer working for BBN, a defense contractor and pioneering technology company, Crowther played a major role in building the Advanced Research Projects Agency Network (ARPAnet), which laid the foundations for the internet. He was a preternaturally calm man known for his quiet and exacting demeanor, but the turmoil of separation—not only legally from his wife, but physically from his two school-age daughters—left him in an unfamiliar state of unrest.[22] Perhaps hoping to direct this energy back into a realm where he felt safe and competent, Crowther leveraged his unique set of skills and interests in a project that few other people in the world would have had the ability or technological access to accomplish: He made a videogame.

Within certain circles, Crowther achieved godfatherly fame for this creation, known variously as *Adventure* (which hints at how few games existed at the time, that he could freely claim such a generic title), *Colossal Cave Adventure* (a later, more specific attribution) or simply *ADVENT* (the game file's original name, truncated because of technological restraints).

In some ways Crowther represented the archetypal computer nerd: mathematically brilliant, minimally verbal, unwilling to don anything but sneakers to even the most formal of functions, such as presenting ARPA to high-level officials at the Pentagon (the sole occasion for which Crowther reportedly wore dress shoes was his wedding).[23] He could also be anomalous, an individual who did not cleanly fit into what would become the generic template of his profession. When contemplating a programming problem, Crowther's mind worked best while performing chin-ups on any nearby door frame, which doubled as a tensile-strength exercise for his great passions: caving and rock climbing. The Mammoth Cave system in Kentucky, containing a subsystem known as Colossal Cave, was one of his favorite sites, and became the inspiration for his groundbreaking game.[24] There was no graphical interface to *Adventure:* scenes and actions were described solely through prose. The game began: "You are standing at the edge of a road before a small brick building. Around you is a forest. A small stream flows out of the building and down a gulley."[25] Typing "help" into the parser provided some modicum of instruction to the uninitiated player, which was basically anyone but Crowther: "Somewhere nearby is Colossal Cave, where others have found fortunes in treasure and gold, though it is rumored that some who enter are never seen again. Magic is said to work in the cave. I will be your eyes and hands. Direct me with commands of 1 or 2 words."[26] Players would then input commands for the game to interpret, which determined what scene or action would next be displayed through descriptive text. Possible player commands might be "go west," "get lamp" or "open grate," depending on what was happening at any given point. Unusual or overcomplicated commands would be met with the game regretfully stating that it did not understand. Should frustration compel the player to vent by typing an expletive into the parser, the game would reply with the admonishment, "Watch it!"

This method of interacting with a computer program was revolutionary, as it required no technical knowledge; the player used normal language to hold a conversation with the game. By mimicking the back-and-forth dialogue that would occur between a player and human "dungeon master" in a tabletop role-playing game like *Dungeons & Dragons*—with which Crowther was very familiar—the people to whom he showed *Adventure* were often fooled into thinking the game was powered by a robust artificial intelligence. In Crowther's view, his creation was little more than a mindless collection of data tables, but he delighted at the trickery.* Having feverishly assembled the game over the course

---

* This could be seen as a rudimentary passing grade for Turing's famous litmus test, which posited that any computer program that could fool a person into thinking it was intelligent had, for all intents and purposes, achieved intelligence.

of several weekends, sharing it with colleagues, his sister, and his children, Crowther promptly lost interest and abandoned it.

In many subsequent interviews and articles, Crowther would say that he wrote *Adventure* to provide his daughters with something fun to do with him on visiting days—but one need not be a trained psychoanalyst to consider that more may have been going on beneath that conscious surface. Eight-year-old Sandy and five-year-old Laura found the game frustrating;[27] as lay-friendly as the system was relative to other computer programs, it was not particularly child-friendly. The game's fantasy-inspired elements, such as a pesky dwarf who throws axes at the player and curses when he misses, could feel frightening and sinister even to adult players.* And caving, the game's focus, was a passion belonging to Crowther (and, notably, his ex-wife), not his children. In 1975, Crowther was living in Massachusetts: a long way from Kentucky and just as far from the halcyon days of a stable, contented family life. A speculative take on *Adventure* might cast it less as a toy for his children than as a powerful, unconscious drive toward catharsis—the release of seemingly irresolvable tension that built up in the wake of his divorce. Perhaps Crowther wanted to go back, to undo his pain, to recreate in the digital world what had so fulfilled him and his ex-wife, but in a form imbued with magic and difficult to complete: immune to the patina of change and

---

* There is an unfortunate overlap of terms in games and psychotherapy when it comes to the word "fantasy." In games, as in literature, fantasy typically refers to the specific genre embodied in J. R. R. Tolkien's writing: a medieval-like setting filled with magical creatures such as elves, orcs, and wizards. In psychotherapy, particularly psychoanalytic psychotherapy, "fantasy" describes the ubiquitous human tendency to intermingle conscious and unconscious thoughts. We might say, for example, that Crowther's use of the dwarf, a staple of the fantasy genre, represented a psychological fantasy of how he viewed himself post-divorce: frustrated, frustrating, and trapped in a dark cave of his own design.

loss, the inevitability of time moving forward and things falling apart. He was amused, maybe even envious, that a game utilizing only a fraction of his programming ability could deceive others into thinking the brain behind it was real, as the swapping of fantasy and reality is what someone in the grip of mourning often most wants—and is most unable to achieve—for himself.

There is no direct evidence that *Adventure* was consciously built as a means for Crowther or his children to work through the pain of divorce. What is better established is that the return to a curated, embellished version of the past left his daughters frustrated and Crowther himself bored. And yet there was a kernel of inspiration in Crowther's work that transcended his personal reasons for creating it and resonated with his peers, those white-collar men who saw in computers the possibility of a new kind of creative expression. It wasn't only *Adventure*'s blend of the real and fantastical that caught people's imaginations, but the sense it gave that in an insular community filled with smart people, one of the smartest had applied himself not toward scientific advancement or financial gain but an emotional experience. A palpable aspect of Crowther's inner world was felt in small measure each time that little dwarf tauntingly hurled an axe at the player; Crowther's passion was reconstituted as the thrill of victory after the player had conquered the perils and puzzles of Colossal Cave. Crowther had put himself into the game, and in playing it others could locate the truth of his experience in themselves.

It is not surprising, then, that decades before online virality entered the lexicon, *Adventure* went viral. Shortly after he had stopped working on the game, Crowther left a copy on his work computer and went on vacation to Alaska; by the time he returned it had been discovered, copied, and played by countless students and programmers at the select institutions connected to ARPA's proto-internet.[28] Discovering and sharing games in this way carried an electric—and illicit—thrill. Game files would regularly be purged by system administrators wary of resources being levied toward recreational use, which meant that the deceptive preservation and transmission of these files (renaming them with banal titles that might pass unnoticed beneath the watchful eye of an official) became an integral part of what it meant to be a member of this earliest iteration of an online gaming community. Around 1977, a Stanford University graduate student named Don Woods was introduced to *Adventure* by a friend who found a copy on a computer in the medical school.[29] Woods requested that *Adventure* be surreptitiously transferred to the computer on which he had an account: appropriately enough, in the artificial intelligence lab. Woods was instantly enamored of the game and reached out to Crowther, asking if he might be willing to share the game's source code and permit Woods to further develop it. Crowther agreed without compunction; he had already lost personal interest in the project and any commercial viability for computer games was then unthinkable. Woods greatly expanded the original version of *Adventure*, unmooring it from Crowther's faithful recreation of Kentucky geography and imbuing it with more fantasy elements—including a troll and a dragon—and a more player-friendly vocabulary system.

Woods's increased use of the fantasy genre was particularly well timed, striking a chord with his computer-savvy ilk who had already turned to literature like Tolkien's *Lord of the Rings* trilogy and tabletop games like *Dungeons & Dragons* for entertainment and, even more, respite. The desire to escape into unreal worlds was growing exponentially at a time when reality was beginning to feel particularly inescapable: the dissolution of free-love utopianism, the seething aftermath of an intractable war in Vietnam, and the mounting threat of global nuclear armament all served to sharpen the appeal of ducking into a fictional, simplified environment.[30] While the updated version of *Adventure* could at times be more frustrating than Crowther's original (Woods added, for instance, a wandering pirate who would steal all the player's accumulated treasure if the two crossed paths), it better wielded the digital world's capacity to bend reality in order to provide the player with catharsis—something that eluded Crowther alone, trapped as he was in a need to faithfully reconstruct the past. When the player faced off with Woods's dragon, the tongue-in-cheek solution was the command "Kill dragon." The computer would respond, perplexed: "What with? Your bare hands?"[31] If the player simply confirmed by typing "Yes," he would be informed that the deed was done: He had slain the mighty beast.

This sequence—absurd and empowering, obvious and opaque—captures why the Woods update of *Adventure* went even further than the original and would serve as a launch pad for a new generation of game-makers. Solving the dragon puzzle was akin to reading the mind of the man who wrote it—sharing a nod and a wink across time and space. American popular culture was focusing on the veneration of the individual and distrust of institutional authority, and the bright young men at the forefront of computing found themselves with no cause to fight for and no obvious justification for feeling frustrated or listless. Early games like *Adventure* functioned as digital inside jokes, the insiders being this growing cabal of quietly disaffected young men: unassuming sorts from socially acceptable backgrounds, of socially acceptable ethnicities, well educated and technically skilled, who accepted the financial and occupational success their privileged status wrought in exchange for the forfeiture of any sense of cultural identity. By the late 1970s the elitism of computer programming had given way to its industrialization: There was money to be made and wars to be won, after all, and the men who worked computers needed to be as reliable as the computers themselves. One of the reasons that few people outside of videogame history buffs have heard the name Will Crowther is because he and his colleagues at BBN (architects of arguably the single most significant technological innovation of the modern era in the form of the internet) toiled in relative obscurity. By all reports Crowther loved working on the ARPA network for its programmatic challenges, yet he was also a pacifist by nature who suddenly found himself a nameless cog in the great machine of the United States Department of Defense during the shameful last days of its most controversial quagmire. Perhaps his wearing sneakers to the Pentagon was more than a personality quirk; the mildest form of defiance, the kind of passive-aggressive gesture that characterized not only Crowther but those he inspired, who preferred to express their true feelings in code rather than spoken words.

Games, then, were a rare sanctuary for folks whose livelihood depended on sticking to the straight and narrow of deference and a good work ethic. Games were open secrets, widely shared among a small, homogeneous community while shielded from the disapproving gaze of institutional, cultural, or moral authority; worlds hiding in plain sight.

IT WAS 1978 when Warren Robinett grew tired of hiding. He'd been ecstatic to be hired at the California-based videogame company Atari the previous year: Their smash-hit *Pong* made the company an instant household name in 1972. But if Robinett thought that a career in game development would help him eschew the paternalism of working as a computer programmer for governments or more serious businesses, he quickly discovered how mistaken he was. Shortly after Robinett arrived at Atari a change in management left the corporate reigns in the hands of a man named Ray Kassar, who became notorious for his bottom-line focus, his Ivy league air of superiority, and marked distrust of his employees.[32] Kassar imposed strict security measures around the Atari offices to protect what he saw as proprietary and economically valuable assets;* gone were the days of free exchange among like-minded programmers, eager to hack into and improve each other's work. Kassar also feared giving individual game designers too much credit in case it put the company in the disadvantageous position of having to either negotiate higher salaries or risk having its talent poached by competitors. Kassar implemented a policy that no programmer could publicly promote his contributions to any Atari title, nor would he receive specific recognition for his work on any company-published materials, including the games themselves.

At the time, Robinett had been working sporadically on a project of personal significance to him: A graphical adaptation of Woods and Crowther's *Adventure*, which Robinett first discovered and played in the same AI lab at Stanford University where Woods implemented his additions. Robinett's interpretation traded the descriptive prose of its progenitor for a more visceral, action-oriented experience. Rather than engaging in typed conversation with the computer, the player directly controlled an on-

---

* Not an inaccurate assessment, given that Kassar would take Atari from $75 million to $2 billion in sales within three years.

screen character, represented by a small square that could move throughout a series of rectangular rooms as seen from a top-down perspective. The goal was to find a chalice deep within the game's dungeon and return it to the castle above, all while collecting keys and other useful items and contending with various creatures such as a hyperkinetic bat and—raising the ante on Woods—not one but three dragons. The size and scope of *Adventure*'s map, as well as its emphasis on completing an overarching quest rather than achieving a high score, placed it on a more ambitious plane than most contemporary commercial games, including those in Atari's line-up. This was in large part due to its source material: Robinett was attempting to translate work built on incredibly powerful computers, such as those at BBN and Stanford University, onto the comparatively pitiful home console microprocessing capacity of Atari's Video Computer System, or VCS.*

That Robinett had to use an electronic key that tracked his movements throughout the Atari offices was grudgingly tolerated, if anathema to the quietly anarchic leaning he shared with many of his peers. But he couldn't bear the idea of his name being omitted from *Adventure* upon its release and all credit going to the nebulous corporate entity of Atari, Inc. Following in the footsteps of those who created the work that had inspired him, Robinett opted not to address his complaints in the physical space of Kassar's office. Instead, he chose to sort things out privately in virtual space, where there was no hierarchy—only the line that divided those who understood the digital world from those who did not.

Robinett created a secret room in the game, one that could only be found through a most labyrinthine and unintuitive proce-

---

* This system is more commonly known now as the Atari 2600; the renaming occurred in 1982 after a more advanced system, the Atari 5200, was released.

dure. The player would have to use a magic bridge (one of the objects that could be carried by the player's character in the game) to enter a small room hidden within a large maze. In that room the player would have to find and click on a single pixel—which Robinson called "the dot"—masked within a wall made up of identically colored pixels, in order to pick it up. With the dot in hand, the player needed to proceed to a different arbitrary wall located in a different part of the game, which the dot would magically allow the player to walk through. Finally, within this most obscure of places, pixels on the screen were arranged to form the words "Created by Warren Robinett" using every hue the VCS's primitive palette could accommodate. "I wanted my name in colored lights," Robinett would later say.[33]

In the tradition of games being defined by paradox, this silly form of self-aggrandizement was also a legitimate rebellion. Not only did Robinett violate Kassar's policy, but his cheeky secret room took up 5 percent of the overall storage on *Adventure*'s Atari cartridge, which was a physical object that was expensive to produce. He told no one of what he'd done, including coworkers who might have been sympathetic; being found out would undoubtedly have resulted in being fired. Robinett had to be satisfied simply knowing his name was in there, if next to undiscoverable.

Though the defiance's existence depended on the obsessive mind-set of the tech-savvy to be discovered, this only took until 1980—a year after *Adventure* was released to commercial success and a year after Robinett left Atari. A twelve-year-old boy wrote to Atari to inquire about the strange room he'd found after messing around for a long time within the game. As the game was already mass-produced and Robinett was no longer with the company, Atari forgave its policy and pushed news of the discovery to the nascent gaming press, for whom this was a sensational scoop.

The magazine *Electronic Games* dubbed Robinett's deep secret an "Easter egg," a term that endures to the present day.[34] Easter eggs helped define who would gravitate toward the new medium and how they would engage with it. Companies saw the promise of secrets as an enticement to consumers, while developers understood the intent behind Robinett's pioneering prank: Easter eggs could be a means to put into the game those jokes, ideas, and parts of themselves that would otherwise never pass the scrutiny of corporate oversight. Because these secrets were not official features of the game but artifacts for only the most ardent virtual explorers—and because most of the top brass at games companies didn't have the technical knowledge to comb source code for questionable material if they wanted to—there were, effectively, no rules. Just as games left the ivory tower and entered the average home, they were quietly inviting a special kind of player: one who was interested in not only playing the game, but playing the *other* game hidden inside it—the shadow game defined not by system, character, and setting but the inky depths of the game designer's uploaded unconscious.

Many of the Easter eggs of the 1980s, '90s, and early 2000s followed in Robinett's footsteps, with developers taking the opportunity to sardonically congratulate themselves or poke fun at a game's supposed seriousness. If a player typed "beam me" into the parser of 1988's *King's Quest IV: The Perils of Rosella** (a graphical adventure in the vein of *The Black Cauldron*) she would be

---

* It is worth noting that this game was designed by Roberta Williams, who helped pioneer the adventure genre that I loved as a child. She was one of only a few women in the 1980s and '90s who occupied a leadership role in game design for major commercial releases.

instantly transported from the game's medieval setting to a *Star Trek*–inspired lounge populated by pixel-art facsimiles of various people who worked on the game. The *Silent Hill* series was famous for including absurdist secret endings that pierced the somber veil of its titles. (The Dog ending of *Silent Hill 2,* for instance, featured James discovering that his nightmare had been orchestrated by a Shiba Inu dog operating behind a *Wizard of Oz*–like control panel.)

Due to the narrow sociocultural band of individuals making and subsequently playing games, however, much of the content expressed through early Easter eggs took the form of heterosexual male gratification—a practice that reached a fever pitch in the 1990s and early 2000s but persists in some corners of the market today. Many forgettable titles for long-defunct consoles, such as 1991's *Rings of Power* (Sega Genesis/Mega Drive) and 1994's *The Apprentice* (Philips CD-i) still pop up in historical conversations of gaming due to their featuring secret codes that unlocked images of naked women—tickling the fancy of both the developers and their presumed like-minded audience. That these titles were chiefly marketed toward children and adolescents made such Easter eggs all the more salacious; playgrounds were abuzz with boys trading rumors of how to unlock a game's most taboo doors, then racing home to discover if, in fact, they had tricked their parents into buying them disguised pornography for Christmas. Games were portals not just to the virtual worlds they represented on their most superficial level, but into the strange machinations of adult sexuality—or, at least, a very particular vision of it.

As the internet grew, so did online communities centered on games and, as a result, hacks and secrets began to sprout and spread from beyond game developers themselves. Fans with programming skills could build patches or plumb the source code of existing titles to impose a shadow world onto a game that initially had none. The release of *Tomb Raider* in 1996—which positioned Lara Croft as a tantalizing sexual object to its target straight, male player, enticing but never pornographic—was followed quickly by an underground patch that, when tracked down in the back corners of the internet and installed in the proper file folder, made Croft appear naked throughout the game.

The pleasure that came from installing the so-called "Nude Raider" patch was a double-edged sword, marked by the glee of subverting authority and the shame of violating an unspoken social rule. The player had circumvented the game developer's desire to let you get close but not too close to Croft but, in defying that boundary, the player relegated himself to the fringe of an already marginalized sect of society increasingly referred to as "gamers."*

Sex and aggression: the two primary energies of the unconscious, according to Freud.[35] Games offered unfettered access to them, bound within an interactive digital world set apart from the disapproving judgment of society (or parents), to a depth

---

* The instances in which games served to gratify taboo fantasy for those willing to wend through backdoors and alleyways are too numerous to list. Another famous example, for the sake of illustration, is the "Hot Coffee" mod for 2004's *Grand Theft Auto: San Andreas.* The game's developers designed a sex simulator that they cut from the finished game . . . but left intact within the game's source code. Whether this was oversight or a silent invitation for intrepid hackers remained unclear, but regardless "Hot Coffee" was unearthed and became widely available for download in 2005. It prompted a media frenzy, product recalls, and legal actions: one of many occasions when the shame around gaming was magnified in the public eye.

and intimacy that no other widely available media ever had. This proved magnetic for a heterosexual male audience being raised in environments that, at least on the surface, espoused increasingly politically correct attitudes, decrying sexism and misogyny and promoting intersectional inclusivity. Games became a place to cathartically release the rage and entitlement that was no longer seen as acceptable in public life.

A gaming boys' club rose insidiously from the earliest days of computing and blossomed during the explosion of the commercial games industry. As games moved online, allowing players across physical space to exist in the same virtual worlds together, a vicious us-versus-them culture developed. Members of the self-appointed reigning class were defined in part by their expertise—anyone who hadn't mastered a game was derogatorily dubbed a "noob"—but above all by their being straight, white men (and boys). Racist, misogynistic, and homophobic epithets were not just commonplace during gaming sessions and in online spaces devoted to games, they were endemic to how the community functioned. Appropriate to gaming's history, this culture was an open secret; those regarded as outsiders either had to keep their heads down and accept relegation to second-class citizenry (which often meant suffering chronic written and verbal abuse, among other indignities) or abandon the space altogether.

By the late-2000s and 2010s, however, the global connectivity of the internet also permitted communities outside the gaming mainstream (which was, ironically, still seen as fringe by the broader mainstream outside of gaming) to coalesce, which in turn led to a sudden increase in the visibility of those who played, made, and wrote about games. It became undeniable that games were supported not only by a homogeneous group of stereotypical "gamers," but by a diverse, far-reaching community.* The skeletal structure of games as hidden gardens filled with even more deeply buried treasure had appealed for years to a variety of people on the margins of society—from gender and racial minorities to those living with physical disabilities and chronic illness—who typically felt being seen was akin to being shamed. Historically, the only faction with an audible voice had been descendants of the original boys' club, but now a conversation was developing around games as an art form, suggesting that they might offer more than immediate gratification of unconscious desire but could also be utilized to explore complex aspects of the human experience—from love to grief to alienation and beyond—and encapsulate a greater band of humanity itself, beyond the singular line of white, heterosexual, male cisgendered life. Attention from mainstream media outlets and the ubiquity of games-ready devices like iPhones exposed a swath of people far outside the gaming norm to the medium for the first time.

Some members of the old guard did not take this sea change lying down. They raised the stakes of what it meant to be part of gaming's present and future community to a terrifying degree, bringing the shadowed history of games into the searing light of day under the banner of a movement called Gamergate.

✳

---

* Solid demographic data about who plays games remains at a rudimentary stage, but the evidence that exists strongly suggests the image of a young, male gamer is more subjective cultural perception than fact. For instance, in 2017 the Entertainment Software Association released a report finding that more adult women endorse playing games (31 percent of the total game-playing population) than boys under eighteen years (18 percent).[36]

By the end of August 2014, Zoe Quinn, an independent games developer, feared for her life. She'd recently been "doxxed," a practice of online passive-aggression in which an individual's real-life information—from name and address to financial details and social security number—are posted, with the intent of not-so-gently encouraging others to use that information to harass the individual. After countless phone calls, emails, and texts that escalated from vague insults to detailed threats of rape and murder by anonymous men who knew where she lived, Quinn decided to leave her home and stay with a friend.[37]

The spark that set off such abuse was, on the surface, a sordid and meandering post on the message board site 4Chan, written by Quinn's ex-boyfriend, in which he accused her of romantic involvement with a games journalist that was "unethical," given her position as a developer. Of course, as we have seen, the surface is rarely where the truth of games resides. Quinn's ex actually incited a virtual mob of self-designated gamers to target his former girlfriend for motives both easy for anyone to understand—a jilted lover feeling powerless and emasculated before a woman who rebuffed him—and oddly particular to the gaming community: Quinn (along with writer Patrick Lindsey and musician Isaac Schankler) had recently released a text adventure game called *Depression Quest.*

As the name might suggest, *Depression Quest* was not fun to play—nor was it intended to be. The player assumed the role of a person struggling with acute clinical depression and was presented with descriptions in prose of her life and surroundings (à la Woods and Crowther's *Adventure*) before being asked to select what she would like to do next. The decision points could be as mundane as whether or not to get out of bed, but they were made weighty and disturbing by how the game's system reflected the character's illness. Options which might have appealed to the player but felt impossible to her character were displayed but greyed out, such as "Shake off your funk and go have a good time with your girlfriend" in response to being invited to a night out. If the character's depression worsened, fewer healthy choices were selectable. The player could attempt to slowly steer her character toward beginning therapy and taking antidepressant medication, which would help to open new options, but no pathway through the game yielded a conclusive, happy ending. Its epilogue, in which Quinn and her collaborators directly addressed the player, stated: "Like depression itself, *Depression Quest* does not have an end really. There is no neat resolution to depression. . . ."[38] The game was not designed as an escape from the harshness of reality but as a virtual simulation of it, which the developers hoped might stoke more open conversation about mental health and illness back in the real world.

Why, exactly, was a group of young games-playing men so angry about *Depression Quest*? The question has been difficult to approach, as doing so demands an empathic stance toward individuals not easy to empathize with, prone as they were and are to freely issuing threats of rape and murder. The absurd rallying cry that Gamergate was a matter of ethics* was shown to be as thin as tissue paper as the online abuse spread on social media platforms like Twitter to target other individuals—often female, transgendered, and/or non-white—against whom no charges of unethical behavior were levied. Feministic games critic Anita

---

* The pretext was that Quinn's game garnered undue attention because of her personal connection to a single journalist—a claim that was discredited in short order, but by then the Gamergate engine was already firing at full blast.

Sarkeesian had a speaking engagement cancelled due to a bomb threat. Multiple game developers quit the industry entirely out of frustration or fatigue from incessant harassment.

To look first, again, at the surface: The grievance expressed by Gamergate folks seemed to be that Quinn and others represented an approach to gaming deemed too serious; that games should be left as fun diversions not subject to artistic exploration or criticism. Yet this attitude failed to justify the nasty personal attacks—often charged with unregulated expressions of sexualized violence—that defined the movement. If a small, independently published project like *Depression Quest* were simply not to these men's tastes, couldn't they simply ignore it? If what it truly represented to them, however, was an invasion of their shadow world—the uploaded unconscious buried in an egg beneath decades of insidious elitism and exclusion—then Quinn's work would be seen as nothing less than an act of war.

The Gamergate contingent was hard to quantify amid the murkiness of online identities; they likely represented a minority of even the legacy gaming community, but one that was blisteringly loud on social media, and their sentiments fell in line with the caricature of "gamers" that had existed in public perception for years. The movement placed a firm political stamp on what it meant either to call someone, or to self-identify, as a gamer: more than ever it became a signifier that not only was one devoted to the medium but had a particular vision of what games should or should not depict and who should or should not be permitted to play and discuss them.

In truth, this was a specific group of men with a shared psychological dependency on games as a means to explore and expel inner fantasies—especially of sexuality and aggression—in ways that seemed unavailable elsewhere in the modern world. These men may have consciously expressed the wish for games to be "just for fun," but there was a deeper need being satisfied, one steeped in the gaming world's designation as a space where members of the majority could vent rage without fear of reprisal, and without consideration for contemporary social values. *Depression Quest* looked squarely at psychological pain and social dysfunction through a medium traditionally leveraged to flee those same phenomena; the game symbolized a larger progressive movement that had been building for years and which, to some, sounded like a death knell for the bombastic hybridization of sex and violence found in many games (or surreptitiously added later through fan-made modifications). If gaming was no longer a restrictive boys' club, how would those who needed it to be just that find release? Where could their shame seek safe harbor now?

From a psychoanalytic perspective, desiring a safe place to express the socially inexpressible is not a wholly bad thing. After all, denying taboo thoughts and feelings due to fear of being shamed does not make those thoughts and feelings disappear, it simply blocks conscious access to them and opens the door to impulsive, unconsciously motivated forms of release. Space in which all aspects of the self are permitted to exist in the open, such as a psychotherapist's office, can allow one to experience and appraise his unconscious consciously, which is an essential step toward achieving greater self-knowledge and change. But awareness is only that: a step, necessary but insufficient. Reconciling fantasy with reality and unconscious with conscious (an important part of the "analysis" in psychoanalysis) means not only being aware of but taking responsibility for the entirety of ourselves in order to feel freer in our ability to choose who we are and how we want to treat ourselves and others. This is the admittedly more difficult step (particularly without adequate support) that adherents of Gamergate seemed collectively frightened to attempt.

Instead, they trapped themselves (and continue to do so, as the movement endures in various forms) in a loop of unfulfilled gratification, using games to release sexual and aggressive tensions without exploring the meaning of those tensions—and viciously attacking anyone deemed a threat to their ability to do so—only to have them build up again and again. Catharsis, in and of itself, is not curative; it is also necessary to understand the drive to catharsis.

The process of making gaming a safe and inclusive space for all is ongoing. But it is important not to throw out the baby with the bathwater: Though many games and players once became obsessed with mindless, uncritical gratification, that should not obscure the present and future value that games hold as a space to explore unconscious fears and desires. The archaeological nature of games—in which surface exploration impels the player to dig deeper, learn the tricks, find the secrets, and even dive into the code of the game itself—is a unique quality born out of gaming's unique history that in turn offers unique insight into the psychology of the player. The burdens of history that must be sloughed off are the long-standing incuriosity around why we play games and, above all, the shame associated with doing so. Shadows, once brought into the light, have the power to redirect energy away from self-loathing and judgment and toward a truer appreciation of gaming's potential.

Chapter 4

Potential

Why do we play videogames?

Why should I be my aunt, or me, or anyone?
—Elizabeth Bishop, "In The Waiting Room"

I FIRST MET THE "GAMER KID," whose name was Jack, on an unseasonably warm afternoon in late October. My office was a far cry from the sanctuary I'd known as a patient with Dr. Lovett: His curated books and furniture were replaced by a small box of a room set aside for trainees featuring the linoleum flooring and sickly yellow walls that, for reasons that have always escaped me, embody the design scheme of most New York hospitals. I placed a couple of framed photographs taken by my girlfriend at the time on the walls in an attempt to disrupt the generic, institutional feel of the space, but there was little I could do about the uncomfortable plastic chairs or the porthole window that, depending on the time of day, provided either no discernible natural light or shone a sunbeam directly in the patient's face.

Jack appeared sweaty and disheveled when I found him in the waiting room, which I initially attributed to the hot weather. He was a relatively average-looking young white man of twenty-one years with a mop of light brown hair and matching eyes, slightly overweight and dressed in a T-shirt so tight as to suggest that his being overweight was a recent development. Across his face were several faint but distinctive scars, the telltale remains of severe adolescent acne.

I showed him into my office and we sat down. My approach to psychotherapy, born out of my experience with Lovett and my subsequent years of professional training, was (and is) centered around creating a space of safe ambiguity, in which the patient's mind takes priority over my agenda. As a result, I was in the habit of allowing a pregnant pause at the start of a session in which the patient might take the reins, rather than relying on me to set a course. I would later come to appreciate that the anxiety of a first session can be so acute for a patient that asking him to begin without guidance forges a space that feels ambiguous but unsafe—and is more likely to be traumatic than therapeutic. Swimming comfortably in the pool of uncertainty requires acclimation over multiple sessions, sometimes for months, and wading into the water is always preferable to being thrown in. These days I take a fairly active role in steering the first few sessions with a new patient and take pains to name the unease that beginning treatment can evoke as the patient learns how to be in the unique space. Thanks to well-intentioned inexperience, however, I now sat across from Jack and said nothing. His eyes darted around the tiny room.

"I don't know why I'm here," he said.

This is not an uncommon sentiment to hear at the start of treatment, especially from younger patients whose presence may be more the result of insistent parents or teachers than at their own request. But Jack's statement did not ring as one of youthful defiance: he sounded genuinely confused. I felt an urge to remind him of his purpose as I understood it from my colleague's intake report: family conflict, academic struggles at college, and, of course, his relationship with games. But, once again, I made a conscious effort to refrain from imposing my narrative on his experience and so I held back.

"We can start wherever you think makes the most sense," I said.

Where Jack started, by all accounts, made no sense. He began speaking at a rapid clip about his older brother Griffin, who Jack alternately described as his tormentor and best friend. Jack said he hoped that psychotherapy would teach him the "mental brain skills" needed to coach his brother toward "a more productive life."

"I'm not sure I understand," I cut in during a brief break in Jack's barrage of words. It was my turn to feel confused. "Who do you think needs help: You or your brother?"

"I don't know!" Jack cried, and then he smacked his open palm to his forehead with enough force to make me start, as though he were trying to knock loose something inside. Another pause—this one less driven by theoretical intention than my simply not knowing what to do. Jack pointed to one of the photographs I'd placed on the wall: a clearing within a thick North Carolina wood, in the middle of which sat an empty wooden bench. "My head feels like that," he said.

"How so?" I asked.

He winced, shook his head, and laughed. "I don't know. I don't know."

By the end of the session, I was even more convinced that use of the "gamer kid" moniker had been problematic. I now feared my colleague, in presuming that someone who played games would be a bit weird, had overlooked signs of a thought disorder:

a serious condition in which an individual is unable to coherently organize and think his own thoughts, and a diagnostic criterion for schizophrenia. Jack's disheveled appearance, odd use of language, and subjective sense of confusion all seemed to support this idea. Maybe games had nothing to do with this; they were just a distraction from a severe psychiatric disorder that would require antipsychotic medication and, presumably, a more experienced therapist to treat.

I spoke to a supervisor about my concerns, feverish in my insistence that this case had been mislabeled and thus inappropriately assigned to me. She listened patiently, then urged me to slow down. Wasn't I rushing to call Jack psychotic in the same way my colleague had rushed to classify him as a gamer—to avoid curiosity about him and hope he became someone else's problem? This observation was particularly striking given that, even if Jack did have a psychotic disorder, treating him would have been well within my professional competency; working with such patients had been a significant part of my clinical training to date, yet my first reaction had been that I was in over my head. Next, I spoke with my colleague who had first interviewed Jack. Since the infamous staff meeting we'd gotten together and talked through the vague animosity I felt about her use of the phrase "gamer kid"; we were on good terms again, even if we still did not see eye to eye on the matter. She listened to my description of my first session with Jack with an astonished look on her face. "That wasn't my experience of him at all," she told me. "He was socially awkward, sure, and I got the sense that he might have felt embarrassed talking about certain things with a woman. But he had no problems answering the intake questions. He seemed excited to share information, even eager to impress me."

One of the most important things for a psychotherapist to keep in mind is the distinction between state and trait. Whether a feature of someone's psychology tends to emerge only under certain conditions (state-based) or is present regardless of outside factors (trait-based) can have dramatic effects on how that person's strengths, difficulties, and diagnosis are understood and treated. I had assumed based on a single meeting that Jack's jumbled way of thinking and speaking represented a trait, a chronic problem that persisted across time and space; a thought disorder. But given my lack of data, I'd had no basis on which to draw such a conclusion. It was just as likely—if not more likely, given the relative rarity of severe psychotic disorders in the general population—that Jack's disorientation was a more transient state brought on by situational factors. Say, for instance, a frighteningly ambiguous psychotherapy session, particularly coming off the heels of an intake interview that had been focused and structured.

That Jack had struggled to cope in an organized way with the openness of our meeting alluded to more chronic problems with identifying and managing his emotions, but I had been shockingly premature in presuming that how I saw Jack one time must be how he always was.* A thought disorder diagnosis was not off the table, per se, but he and I simply needed to spend more time together. Jack's behavior could not be made meaningful by looking at him alone—our relationship informed how he'd engaged with the space of the office, the time of the session, the world of psychotherapy.

---

* I also made the inverse error when initially assuming that Jack's unkempt appearance had been a temporary state due to the weather. Regardless of whether one projects health or illness onto someone else, it's still only a projection until enough actual data comes in.

In subsequent sessions with Jack, I took a more directive approach than was usual for me at the time. I would start with an open-ended question ("What's on your mind?") rather than silence; when pauses stretched out for long periods or Jack seemed to be losing the thread of our conversation, I would gently guide him back to where it seemed he'd gone off-trail ("You were talking about studying for mid-terms—how's that going?"). Eventually I tried pointing out Jack's more unconscious processes to him ("Did you notice that as soon as you started talking about Griffin, your speech got fast and agitated?").

One thing we absolutely did not discuss was games—the very topic that drew me to work with Jack, that made everyone in the clinic believe that I was the right therapist for the job. Why was it so difficult for us to talk about something we both considered important? Jack and I spoke the common language of games (though he didn't know it yet), but still there was an inhibition in me, a fear that it would be untherapist-like to talk about them with a patient. After all, I had never talked about games with my therapist.

I also felt an invisible pressure to crack the mystery of Jack's personality through my knowledge of the gaming world and feared discovering that in reality I had nothing special to offer this young man. Looking back, I think this was a large part of why I reacted the way I did after my first meeting with Jack: I'd spoken up in a staff meeting, been granted the responsibility of Jack's treatment as a result, and was now terrified of disappointing everyone involved, including myself.

IN LIEU OF GAMES we discussed nearly every other element of Jack's daily existence and one notion stood out above all others: Jack lived in a world without boundaries.

Home was a crowded apartment he shared with his parents and adult siblings (twenty-four-year-old brother Griffin and eighteen-year-old sister Claire) in which privacy was unknown, intimacy could not be disentangled from aggression, and contradictions were the norm. Jack might explode at his parents, demanding more privacy and shortly thereafter leave the door open when going to the bathroom. Psychological problems within the family interlocked like a dysfunctional jigsaw puzzle to create an environment of overwhelming chaos. Claire, for instance, who took medication for obsessive compulsive disorder (I always suspected both her diagnosis and treatment were inadequate), had a tendency to bring home objects and furniture she found on the street: a rusted office chair, a frayed wicker side table, a stack of books on infant care. Jack's mother refused to acknowledge that anything might be troubling her beloved youngest child and would not comment on these acquisitions, even as they took up the little free space remaining in the apartment. Jack's father was too physically absent to notice the accumulation and Griffin too depressed (and frequently intoxicated with alcohol) to do anything about it. Jack felt alone in his sense of claustrophobia as the apartment grew ever more cluttered, while the rest of his family behaved as though everything was as it should be.

I had been correct in my assumption that Jack's weight gain was recent, but not in the way I'd expected. He told me that his body constantly fluctuated through periods of relative bingeing and restricting food—I was merely catching him on a binge cycle, the precipitants for which he could not articulate. Jack's clothes were tight because he only had outfits that suited his trimmer phases. He rarely bought new clothes due to his limited income (working part time at a drugstore) and the unpredictability of requesting financial help from his father, who might come home one day with a lavish and unnecessary gift for the family and then days later announce that there would be severe austerity measures in place for the foreseeable future.

Jack's school life had also been chaotic. It was frequently disrupted by his father moving the family every few years to pursue entrepreneurial efforts that never panned out. (His gig when I knew Jack was working as a freelance Bible salesman.) Now settled on Staten Island, south of Manhattan, Jack had no meaningful community ties and his only friends were people he'd met at college, a reputable art school in Manhattan. (Though the school did not offer a specific major in videogame design, Jack was in the vanguard of its interactive media department.) Jack felt a paradoxical kinship with his peers, the first concentrated group of people he had known who were pursuing creative interests, and a profound resentment toward them for both the money he presumed they had that allowed them to live near campus (Jack's one-way commute could stretch up to two hours) and the love and support from their families that such financial backing seemed to imply. His relationships with friends were accordingly contrary, marked by Jack's confusion over the line between closeness and invasion. He might overshare with others about his masturbatory habits in an effort to feel understood, but only succeed in disturbing his friends and pushing them away.

Jack vaguely denied any history of physical or sexual abuse to me, stating that he had "very few memories" before the age of ten, which was also the age that he began a long and compulsive relationship with online pornography. We never unearthed truly buried memories of abuse—a phenomenon that is, in my professional experience, exceedingly rare. As time went on, however, Jack and I would look at certain memories that he'd archived as unremarkable and reconsider them as abusive—for example, periodically being sent to middle school by his parents with no food, money, or shoes as punishment for naughty behavior that was never quite defined.*

During our sessions, Jack would eat, belch, fart, or discuss his bowel movements, which made me feel simultaneously close to and repulsed by him: an experience that mirrored how Jack experienced intimacy. In turn, Jack found my interpretations of his behavior to be accurate but intrusive, as though I were reading his mind. Even what I thought to be relatively benign observations—such as the one mentioned above in which I noted that Jack seemed to grow more anxious when he brought up certain subjects—were regarded as an emotional penetration that felt both unwelcome and masochistically pleasurable to him.

I liked working with Jack but following the swells of his thoughts and feelings often left me dizzy. The strange notion that he was in treatment as a means of helping his brother quickly fell away, replaced by an expressed desire to improve the quality of his relationships and a voracious need to better understand himself—a need he sometimes pursued to the point of becoming overwhelmed, another boundary Jack struggled to keep intact.

During one session a few months into treatment, we returned to the photograph on my wall and his assertion that it in some way represented how he felt on the inside. "So alone, like the bench, but

---

* The veracity of such memories was impossible to verify, and on one hand it seemed plausible that they were more emotionally than factually true. Wouldn't someone at school have noticed if Jack were showing up barefoot every so often? Then again, I also wondered if Jack's father's tendency to relocate the family might have coincided with points at which members of their current community were beginning to notice that something was amiss.

the forest is so crowded, like living with my family," he said, evidencing insight into the tension he often experienced between the desire to be alone and the terror of loneliness. An awareness that he had struck upon something meaningful and true visibly excited Jack—he leaned forward and began tapping his foot—and he seemed unable to stop himself from pushing further, beyond the point that he could hold his thoughts together in a coherent way.

"Who took that photo, anyway?" he asked, his speech speeding up. Then, before I could respond, he said with a prescience that left me dumbstruck: "Was it your wife?"

I had never discussed my personal relationships with Jack and, as I was not married at this point in time, I didn't wear a ring, which made his fantasy of me as a married man all the more notable. That he nevertheless guessed the identity of the photographer with reasonable accuracy (and, I suppose, correctly predicted that I would one day marry her) was the kind of uncanny event that I would come to associate with Jack's extreme degree of boundary diffusion. The ease with which he could lose touch with his sense of self and dissolve into his surroundings—often a terrifying and incoherent experience for him, as I witnessed during our first session—also brought with it a remarkable intuition about other people.* Of course, being in a dissolved state of mind meant that

---

* Other patients I have treated with similar conditions as Jack's (which I name and discuss later in this chapter) have also seemed attuned to an emotional wavelength that those with more developed boundaries have not. One patient dreamed I was having a child the week before I had planned to announce my paternity leave. Another once showed me a drawing that she said was inspired by one of our sessions, and which she "for some reason" chose to do in the style of Edvard Munch—who, unbeknownst to her, was my favorite painter. Such eerie occurrences should not be mistaken as a superpower, however: these patients also frequently misjudge situations or unknowingly project their own feelings onto others, as the fluidity with which they move across the borders of inside and outside is often not under conscious control.

Jack rarely had conscious access to how he intuited the things he did; if you were to ask him he would say that he found other people utterly inscrutable. In fact, feeling more connected to others was one of the most pressing things he wanted to work on in therapy.

Jack continued, "Sometimes I think about you being married. I think I would like to be married someday. I think I would like to be married to you." He winced again; his face seemed suddenly drained of color, overcast with a shadow of shame. "I don't know why I said that, I'm sorry." He laughed nervously and repeated, "I don't know why I said that."

The looseness of his thoughts—unraveled by the intensity of his earlier insight—temporarily blurred Jack's distinction between inside and outside, fantasy and reality. Did he really believe I was married or did he just imagine the possibility that I might be? Did he really have romantic feelings toward me or was that an overly literal interpretation of an untethered stream of consciousness? Upon realizing that he had drifted so far from the normal boundaries of social interaction, Jack was mortified. In the moment I didn't know how to dispel his shame without amplifying it—how to let him know that in our space, this cramped and ugly office, it was OK to voice thoughts that might be regarded as bizarre or inappropriate in other, "normal" places. More than OK, in fact, but useful. Jack's comment surely had multiple meanings worth exploring, one of which spoke to a bond, a connection, that was developing between us. But it was difficult to talk about our relationship without being swept up in the perversity of Jack's inner, unbounded world.

AFTER SEEING JACK for about a year—by which time he was much more comfortable starting off a session unprompted—he began one day: "I'm not sure what to talk about, I haven't been thinking much about my life." I inquired what, then, had been on his mind. He immediately replied, "*Mass Effect.*"

This was not the first videogame that Jack had mentioned in session, but he usually did so in a more offhanded way, couched among other topics that quickly took precedence. My own thoughts on the value and meaning of games had been developing over the preceding year and I felt readier to take on this area of Jack's life that had previously been avoided—especially as he seemed to be serving it up on a silver platter. So, for the first time, in a direct and curious way, I asked him to tell me more about the game he was playing. His body shifted: He sat up straighter, looked me in the eye and started to talk. It occurred to me that what had changed in his demeanor was that he no longer felt in a state of confusion or chaos: we were discussing something about which he felt wholly comfortable.

Mass Effect, the first title in a blockbuster franchise, was initially released for Microsoft's Xbox 360 console in 2007. Jack, due to financial issues that were a constant source of frustration and shame for him, could rarely afford consoles or games when newly released and instead would pick them up for cheap as they approached obsolescence. Here was another way Jack felt isolated from his tech-minded, games-playing peers: He was perpetually reluctant to admit being months or years behind what they were using and playing. Bringing *Mass Effect* into our session was likely motivated in part by the fact that Jack felt unable to share his enthusiasm for it with his friends, out of a fear (whether accurate or misplaced) that they would judge him for only now experiencing a game that they had all played years ago.

Mass Effect put the player in control of Commander Shepard, a veteran soldier, in the year 2183. A high-ranking peacekeeping official had committed treason and Shepard was enlisted by a galactic council to uncover and stop the traitor's unfolding schemes. In the tradition of many Western role-playing games (also known as RPGs), the player could customize Shepard's appearance and abilities from the outset, including gender.* (Owing to the widely regarded superiority of the actor who voiced her, many favored the female version, dubbed FemShep by fans—though Jack played as the male Shepard.) The game involved exploring planets and completing missions both central and ancillary to the main storyline. While some matters were resolved through straightforward tactical combat, many others were handled diplomatically via dialogue in which the player could opt to placate or intimidate others as he saw fit.

At this point in treatment, Jack had demonstrated significant improvement in some areas and relative stagnation in others. After several months of weekly sessions, we had increased to meeting twice per week and the consistency of this schedule had a noticeable impact, even though Jack still found our sessions stressful at times. By committing himself to a specific time and space on a regular basis—and knowing that in that time and space he would be able to express the thoughts and feelings that had accrued since the previous session—Jack became somewhat less reliant on impulsive behavior in his daily life as an outlet for his painful feelings. Impulse, by its nature, is the process of emotion skipping over thought and moving straight into action, and Jack had long struggled with issues of impulsivity.

He had a tendency to punch himself in the arm or slap himself in the face when upset; like many others who engage in so-

---

* "Western" RPGs stand in contrast to Japanese RPGs, which traditionally featured prebuilt player characters.

called self-injurious behaviors, Jack described the physical pain as a kind of release from his emotional strife. But he struggled to put into words what he had been upset about or why the feelings gave way to attacking himself at that specific moment. Because his distress had been resolved in the body and thus bypassed conscious thought, the opportunity to learn was lost, the unthinkable feelings would inevitably return, and the same temporary release would be sought. By symbolizing emotions through language in therapy and thus making them "thinkable," the need to relieve emotional tension through self-harm behavior lessened. This process was often as straightforward as helping Jack label what he was feeling. He might begin a session saying that he had been "feeling a lot" or that he was "all worked up." If by the end of the session he could verbalize that he felt "angry" or "anxious" and perhaps had some notion of what factors were contributing to that feeling, a sense of calm would emerge, brought on by understanding why he felt the way he did. This would mitigate the need to physically harm himself.

Not all impulsivity had been curtailed, however. Jack's episodes of punching and slapping himself, which he tended to do in private moments of distress, had reduced from occurring nearly daily to once or twice per month. He was still prone to abrupt violent outbursts around other people, particularly his family. Jack's aggression typically targeted inanimate objects—he had on multiple occasions smashed plates on the ground or punched a dent in the wall—but also involved wrestling matches with Griffin, which either brother might initiate, and which could quickly get out of hand. Furthermore, Jack continued to experience difficulty at school (he received an incomplete in one of his courses due to feeling paralyzed and failing to complete a final assignment) and still grappled with confusion, resentment, and loneliness toward his tenuous group of friends. He'd developed a deep romantic infatuation with a classmate named Karen, but from session to session I had trouble tracking whether Jack viewed their relationship as close or barely acquainted.

Dynamics within the family had, if anything, grown worse: Griffin had been fired from his job and now rarely left the apartment; to accommodate Claire's hoarding, her parents insisted that she move into Jack's bedroom, which forced him to sleep on the living-room couch. Jack had taken to playing *Mass Effect* late at night when all the others were asleep in their respective bedrooms and he could, through absorption in the game, achieve some semblance of privacy.

Mass Effect invited the player to delve into its dense science fiction universe to whatever depth suited him, offering a plethora of optional missions and lore. Whenever the player came across a new character, species, planet, or technology, relevant information would be added to the "codex," an in-game encyclopedia containing expository details outside the scope of Shepard's focused storyline. No tangible benefit came from taking the time to read up on the fact that the elephantine species known as the *elcor* originated from a high-gravity planet and tended to find long starship journeys uncomfortable, or that the diminutive mole creatures called the *volus* once masterminded a universal banking law that now governed the galactic economy. A player would know these things only if he wanted to know them; if the minutiae of this fictional world felt, for one reason or another, meaningful.

Jack knew everything about *Mass Effect*. In a very real way he struggled to keep the basic elements of his life in coherent order from day to day, but the complex politics, histories, and geographies of the game coalesced seamlessly in his mind and he was able to convey them to me in a relatively cogent fashion. It would have been easy to dismiss Jack's expounding on his fascination with a jellyfish-like species called the *hanar* as nonsense or a waste of time. But it was my impression that Jack was demonstrating a capacity to organize and reflect upon his thoughts—an important skill that was far less apparent when he recounted the latest instance of a shoving match against his brother which, from his point of view, erupted out of thin air.

Regarding the hanar, for instance, Jack was particularly interested in the fact that every member of the species, according to the *Mass Effect* codex, had two names: a public Face Name, and a private Soul Name known only by close relations. He identified with the notion of presenting himself differently in different contexts, but also admired the deliberateness with which the hanar decided who was entitled to what parts of themselves. Jack, conversely, felt he was constantly suppressing shameful aspects of himself around friends—such as his socioeconomic status, his contentious family life and a self-described "need" to watch pornography at least once per day—and would then wallow in those same aspects when at home. Most of the time Jack felt barely in control of what parts of himself he allowed other people to see, and when he became upset or overwhelmed that minimal control would dissipate entirely.

At one point I suggested he wished he had a Soul Name like the hanar, but he insisted it was more than that.

"I wish there was such thing as Soul Names," he said. "I wish people knew that's how it worked. It would make it easier . . ." He paused for a moment, considering. "In *Mass Effect*, every alien group has its *thing*. It's so simple, but there's also so much . . .

so much to learn." Voluminous though it was, Jack seemed to relish that the universe of the game was knowable—and abided by knowable systems—in a way the real world, in his experience, was not.

Perhaps the most compelling and unique aspect of *Mass Effect* was its focus on cultivating relationships. As Shepard explores new planets and becomes increasingly embroiled in galactic intrigue and ancient mysteries, the player assembles a motley crew of human and alien allies. During intermission furloughs aboard their spaceship, the *SSV Normandy,* the player can freely pursue friendships and romantic relationships between Shepard and various other characters by engaging them in optional conversations over the course of the game.*

Considering that a major theme of my sessions with Jack revolved around his feeling unable to engage in relationships, I was struck by how he spoke about his experience with the game in relational terms: how it challenged him, how he pushed back against it, how it made him feel. Jack expressed feeling satisfaction in the pursuit of an in-game romance for its consistency and predictability—qualities that were also beneficial in the context of our therapeutic relationship. He knew that by regularly talking to a crew member he fancied and being kind to her (Jack chose to direct Shepard's affection toward a human gunner aboard his ship named Ashley), his chances of becoming involved with her would incrementally and reliably improve. Jack seemed to be test-

---

* *Mass Effect* was trailblazing in allowing the possibility for FemShep to become romantically involved with a female alien crewmate—though this proved so incendiary among conservative gaming fans and critics that the developers backed off same-sex relationships in the sequel. It was not until *Mass Effect 3* that both gay and lesbian relationships could be pursued if the player so chose.

ing out ways of being—within the safety of *Mass Effect*'s virtual environment—including the idea of building sustained intimate relationships. They carried some of the emotional weight of real life but none of the consequences.

If there were truth in my colleague's initial proclamation that Jack "lacked the basic skills" of people his age—which I now would agree was readily observable in his daily, physical life—it seemed curious that his skills as a game player were not only present but flourishing. Perhaps progress hinged not on discouraging Jack's gaming behavior outright but on understanding his relationship with the game and with the version of himself he inhabited when playing: the distinction and overlap between Jack-as-Shepard and Jack-as-Jack.

To BETTER UNDERSTAND the connection between Jack's virtual and physical selves, I turned to psychoanalytic theory. D. W. Winnicott—an English pediatrician and psychoanalyst practicing in the mid-twentieth century—had already been a significant influence on my development as a clinician and his work seemed especially apt in this case. Winnicott's background in pediatrics directly informed his psychoanalytic interest in how fantasy meets reality, realms through which children tended to pass more freely and unselfconsciously than adults.*

In fantasy, we are masters of the world: our private, internal world. Anything we think can be real there, anything we want to be true is true. While dreaming or daydreaming we might hold conversations with people who, in external reality, are dead or never lived at all. We might imagine ourselves as a different ver-

---

* With the exception, as I discuss later on in this chapter, of adults suffering from borderline and psychotic disorders.

sion of ourselves or someone else entirely; time and space bend to our wills. The caveat to this omnipotence is that in fantasy we are alone: Total control is only possible because our thoughts and feelings reside within us, segregated from the outside world. Reality, conversely, is social: It is the outside world where we learn how things work and develop relationships with other people. Outside of ourselves there is possibility, but also frustration—as we cannot control the thoughts, feelings, and behaviors of others (though we often try).

Experience, according to Winnicott, is the intersection of the two, and learning to tolerate the frustrations of reality without losing one's ability to fantasize is the process of growing up.[39] Facilitating it all are the parents who, Winnicott said, need not be perfect, only "good enough" to help usher the child through development while keeping her sense of both inner and outer worlds intact.[40]

Parents who cannot tolerate their child's distress may fail to teach her that while pain and frustration are inevitable parts of life, such feelings can be confronted and resolved. The child never learns to accept reality—that some things are easy and some impossible, but many things land in between—and she grows up with a sense of extreme vulnerability to the whims of external forces. She might be terrified of anything she cannot directly control (which we typically call generalized anxiety) or, as a means to protect herself, she may refuse to believe that anything truly is outside of her control (which we typically call narcissism).

The inverse failure to be good enough carries its own vicissitudes: This child is made to feel that conforming to the demands of reality is the only way to survive or receive love from her parents. She must abandon the private fantasies that make her feel most like herself in order to please the unyielding outside world. This child grows up to feel that her worth is dependent on the approval of others (which we typically call social anxiety) or she comes to feel so far away from herself that she descends into despair (which we typically call depression).

Children whose upbringings are defined by chaos (such as those with parents who are abusive) may struggle to maintain their sense of the boundary between fantasy and reality. A common scenario that, despite its ubiquity, never ceases to disturb me: a parent abuses his child, then admonishes her for "making him" do it. The rationale makes no sense, because no one can "make" another person beat or rape a child (or adult). The child tries to understand this notion that cannot be understood: Maybe, at her core, she is rotten? After all, she sometimes has angry thoughts about her father—maybe he can read her mind? It is easier for a child to believe that monstrousness lives in her than in her parent, as she is still dependent on the parent to survive. She attempts to become a mind reader herself in order to anticipate her parent's moods, but he is so unpredictable she has trouble distinguishing whether an uneasy internal feeling is based on her or the parent or something else entirely. Over time she may learn to slip into a dissociated fantasy any time abuse is imminent: She has no means to physically extricate herself, so retreating into the sanctuary of her mind is the best available option. Eventually, this happens without any conscious effort and as a coping strategy it becomes generalized to any situation that provokes a sense of danger.

In some cases, this kind of sustained abusive environment can contribute to the development of psychotic disorders like schizophrenia, in which the line between inside and outside is chronically confused (such as mistaking an internal voice as one coming from the outer world, which we call a hallucination). However, most psychotic disorders have high genetic heritability, meaning environmental factors alone are unlikely to cause them. Development is also not a straight line and the introduction of a stable figure in the form of a second parent, teacher, older sibling or therapist can immeasurably help to steer the child back toward a stable sense of herself in the face of soul-rending torment.

The way that gene and environment interact in the development of conditions like schizophrenia and bipolar disorder is complex. Someone with high genetic loading may develop a disorder despite growing up in a relatively safe and stable environment, as might someone with lower genetic loading raised amid chronic abuse. Compounding the question of where severe mental illness comes from is the fact that a parent with untreated mental illness not only passes down genes that may make the child vulnerable to the disorder, but he may also struggle to create a safe environment for the child due to his own inner struggles.

In many cases, however, children like Jack who grow up in chaotic environments marked by poor boundaries continue, as adults, to live unstably at the border between fantasy and reality, which we typically call borderline personality disorder (BPD).* I didn't diag-

---

* Two important caveats: 1) Parental abuse or neglect is not the only pathway to boundary diffusion and BPD. Other traumas that occur within or outside the home, particularly those that happen not once but repeatedly and are not properly addressed and contextualized by caregivers (because they don't know about them or don't know how to seek adequate help), can, over time, also lead a child to grow confused about whether the chaos she experiences is coming from the inside or the outside. 2) My clinical experience, and most research on the development of psychological disorder, is retroactive in nature. By the time I meet a patient she is already suffering and we try to work backwards to understand what factors have contributed to that suffering. In other words, while I strongly believe that someone accurately diagnosed with BPD invariably experienced significant childhood trauma, neither I nor anyone can say that traumatic childhood experience invariably leads to the development of BPD.

nose Jack with BPD because at that time I still held on to a rigid definition of the diagnosis as proffered by mainstream psychiatric thought. Many people, including mental health professionals, regard BPD as a disorder identified only through stereotypical behavior such as self-mutilation and suicidality, which Jack did not display (his tendency to punch and slap himself rarely left a visible mark and so would be deemed a "subclinical" symptom by a dogmatic diagnostician). The common assumption that people with BPD have a proclivity for the emotional manipulation of others similarly did not apply, as Jack was not socially savvy enough to manipulate anyone. Jack also did not seem to suffer from the fear of abandonment typically associated with BPD—he had such a hard time forming relationships in the first place, any anxiety around losing them never had a chance to bubble up into consciousness.

BPD is better regarded as a disorder of traumatic experience in which the patient has grown up to feel that boundaries between inside and outside are permeable and hard to distinguish. This is hardly a novel definition: the very term "borderline" derives from the idea of the condition existing between more organized, "neurotic" ways of being and more disorganized, psychotic ways of being. Psychoanalysts like Otto Kernberg have long regarded BPD as a matter of psychological boundaries over any specific external behavior[41] and psychologists like Peter Fonagy have argued that the disorder is rooted in childhood abuse.[42] These perspectives, however, have been overshadowed by dominant psychiatric manuals and this in turn has contributed to stigma around BPD and misdiagnosis of those who do not display classic symptom presentations. Some evidence suggests these atypical cases (which are not really atypical if you define the disorder properly) may frequently be misdiagnosed with bipolar disorder, a condition of different origins that requires very different treatment.[43] Some practitioners have moved away from the diagnosis of BPD entirely in favor of a newer one called complex post-traumatic stress disorder. While this latter term better captures the connection between chronic early abuse and later psychological turmoil, I still prefer the diagnostic label of BPD for its emphasis on the role borders play in how the disorder manifests.

Jack didn't confuse himself in the real world with himself inside *Mass Effect*,* but his sense of fluidity between the two helped explain why he played. While others might dismiss hours of game-playing as being a waste due to its having no impact on real life, Jack saw less of a difference between living virtually and living physically. If anything, it was in the game that Jack felt more alive. As son, brother, student, patient, Jack often felt confused, ashamed, and unloved. But as Commander Shepard, as *player*....

IF EXPERIENCE FROM WINNICOTT'S perspective was the intersection of fantasy and reality, play was what happened when two or more people experienced something together. This was most obvious when watching children play pretend: One child brings something from the inside to the outside (the thought, I want to be Superman, becomes the declaration, "I'm Superman!") and another affirms the thing to be true and brings her own fantasy into the shared reality (she replies, "OK and I'm Wonder Woman and we have to save the world together!"). Good enough playmates are capable of indulging one another's fantasies of omnipo-

---

* Boundary loss such as that, in which the distinction between fantasy and reality disappears, would be indicative of a psychotic state. Individuals with BPD can dip into such states for brief periods—indeed, anyone is capable of losing touch with reality for a time under extremely stressful conditions.

tence while simultaneously imposing their own reality: The child acting as Superman, running around in a circle, says that he can fly "faster and higher" than his partner.

She counters, "No, we fly the same."

He pauses in his circuit, thinks for a moment and says, "You're right."

Should one or the other refuse to share space and allow the other's experience to commingle with their own, play would end. "You're not being fair!" one might shout before storming off, no longer seeing herself or her friend as superheroes—they're back to being children, one frustrated by the immobility of the other.

Winnicott saw play occurring in situations far beyond such literal accounts. Adults discussing art and ideas could be seen as a form of play. Psychotherapy, in Winnicott's estimation, was often the process of teaching the patient *how to play*, with the therapist assuming the role of the good-enough parent that the patient may have lacked earlier in life. Even a mother feeding her baby could be accurately described as playing: The mother's fantasies of nurturance and the real struggles of breastfeeding intersecting with the baby's (nonverbal) fantasies of being sated and the harsh reality of having to work for his meal. Meeting in the middle, they achieve an emergent playfulness, a bond, a sense of truly being together in the same physical and emotional space; a safe, intermediate space between the singularity of internal experience and the foreignness of external life; a boundaried, mutually accepted playground existing, however fleetingly, between the inside and the outside. Winnicott called it *potential space*.[44]

The purpose of playing in potential space goes beyond having fun: It is the jumping-off point for growth, for health. It teaches us new ways to connect, self-reflect, and feel known. Of course, when Winnicott first wrote about the notion of potential space in the 1950s, videogames did not exist. He likely did not envision that it might one day be a computer simulation, rather than another human being, who could act as the good-enough playmate, indulging and frustrating the player in equal measure. While a BPD diagnosis could retroactively help to explain aspects of Jack's intense relationship with games, the notion of games as potential space carried broader implications. It granted insight into why anyone plays, from the most casual to the most devoted of players.

Games simulate our potential: who we might be and how it might feel to be that way. Players are provided the chance to try out being the altruist or the sadist, the powerful or the powerless and many shades of grey in between. Because the game world is real—but not too real—it invites us to experiment with different versions and parts of ourselves that may seem inaccessible or overwhelming in daily life. And for some, games may represent an invaluable pathway to future growth.

Jack's relationship with *Mass Effect* certainly qualified as play in the Winnicottian sense. His actions in the game weren't mindless or random; on the contrary, as Shepard, Jack took up problems to be solved, learned new skills, and forged new relationships. He did these things well, with purpose and a sense of competency. He welcomed new challenges and spoke fluently of his play, all with minimal anxiety. These were, by any reasonable standard, the kind of benchmarks one would want to see in a healthy young man: purpose, competency, confidence, a desire to learn about the self and form close relationships with others. It just happened that Jack-as-Shepard was further along these developmental lines than Jack-as-Jack. Though even saying it "just happened" to be that way robs the game of its due credit: Game-space gave Jack the sense of safety he needed to explore his potential and realize healthy aspects of himself. The circumstances of his upbringing had been too inconsistent, diminishing, and at times outright abusive for such growth to occur in the physical world, through more socially accepted forms of play.

Looking at Jack through this lens meant that, rather than trying to wean him off games, therapy from this point on would be a process of helping him expand his ability to play from chiefly within the game—where he was presently healthiest—to domains outside it where he still struggled. This was a radical stance to take given how everyone else, from Jack's parents to some of my colleagues and supervisors in the clinic, regarded his game-playing behavior. It seemed to others so obviously problematic, so clearly exerting a harmful effect on his brain. Hadn't games done to Jack the very thing everyone suspected: turned him strange, antisocial, and violent?

After my misunderstanding of Jack at our first meeting, I was learning to slow down before arriving at definitive conclusions. This meant asking a more fundamental question, one that other people's judgments of Jack presupposed. One that, as I would discover, had been written off prematurely by the media, the public, and the scientific community alike.

A question of violence.

Chapter 5

Violence

Do videogames make people violent?

I only know he was my little Alan, and then the Devil came.

—Peter Shaffer, *Equus*

HERE IS THE FEAR: The game seduces.

Like the quietly treacherous vizier whispering in the monarch's ear, the game compels us to act or abstain from action; it steers us toward violence or social withdrawal. Because of the game, everyone's head is seen through crosshairs; real life loses its luster. The game is dangerous, an infectious substance we blindly invite into our homes and minds; it takes us over and makes us lose track of ourselves.

The irony of this long-running hypothesis—that games foreclose thought and, through some sinister alchemy, transform us into something other than what we are—is that it, too, is guilty of foreclosing thought and misrepresenting human nature. By casting people as passive organisms ripe for infestation by the videogame parasite, we abdicate all responsibility for our virtual (and at times physical) behaviors and it becomes impossible to actually understand the phenomena of desensitization and violence inside and outside the gaming world. We are quick to blame games because it is faster, easier, and less demanding of serious thought than asking what our role is in all of this.

The idea that videogames cause real-world violence is one you've likely heard before. More than that, it may feel like a fact, something you *know*. But how do you know it? Try to recall precisely when and where you acquired this knowledge. If you're having trouble, you're not alone—it's a phenomenon that cognitive psychologists refer to as "source confusion." This is the inability to locate the acquisition of semantic information (a fact, or supposed fact) in episodic memory (your lived experience). From the perspective of a psychotherapist, source confusion is one of the most ubiquitous tragedies of the human condition. A lesson is learned earlier in life, then consciously forgotten but continues to exert its influence. Because we lose track of who taught us what, we also forget to question whether a lesson from the past still holds true in the present—or if, in fact, it was ever true.

Just as a patient with BPD may believe unquestioningly that she is empty inside or rotten to the core—because she cannot remember a time when that was not felt to be true (emotional, subjective truth being confused with objective fact)—there is a cultural notion that videogames cause violence because it *feels* like something we know, something that must be true. On some level, and despite my lifetime of playing games without ever erupting into a violent rampage, I, too, believed this to be true for many years. Or, if I didn't quite believe it, I certainly believed other people believed it, which reinforced the shame associated with playing games and the idea that it was a hobby best kept hidden.

Fear of gaming has been collectively internalized over the past four decades, an insidious simmer that reached its boiling point at the turn of the millennium. Public suspicion began in the late

1970s, when major news outlets began haphazardly invoking tabletop role-playing titles like *Dungeons & Dragons* in connection with instances of erratic or self-destructive youth behavior. The *New York Times* and *San Francisco Chronicle* and *Examiner*, among many other papers, printed articles in the '70s and '80s that unambiguously suggested a causal relationship between the structured fantasy play of *D&D* and frightening outcomes like devil worship and suicide.[45] Reading through various examples of these stories highlights an underlying source of the paranoia growing among parents, teachers, and law enforcement: they were disturbed that these "new" games—unlike socially acceptable forms of play such as athletics—took place in nonphysical spaces. As we have seen, games occur uniquely in the potential space shared between the player and the world-builder (a role, in videogames, adopted by the computer rather than a human being). To the parties involved, the experience is imbued with powerful meaning and emotion as fantasy meets reality in a safe, temporary playground. But to an outside observer the activity of play can seem baffling, like trying to see into a black box. A parent watches her child feverishly pressing buttons on a controller while staring at a screen; the act appears to captivate the child, but to the parent—who is privy to neither the virtual space in which the game exists nor the psychological space in which the child derives meaning from the game—the whole endeavor can look like a hollow trance.

The parent doesn't realize it, but her lack of understanding is the start of an unconscious process through which she will project her anxieties about raising a healthy child onto the game. Because the game is opaque to her, it holds an infinite capacity for responsibility that the parent feels unable or unwilling to take on herself. Any troubling behavior that the child demonstrates from this moment forward can be attributed to the corrupting influence of the game. Who can say otherwise? No one knows what's happening in the child's mind, so no one can prove that the game isn't *doing* something to the child's mind.

For decades, all of this was conjecture; a mild concern over what was considered a fringe hobby of certain children and adolescents. The occasional editorials that popped up when a troubled teen did something newsworthy were based on anecdotal evidence and few saw any value in putting the emerging phenomenon of videogames under the scientific microscope. But this attitude changed dramatically after April 20, 1999, the day that Eric Harris and Dylan Klebold murdered twelve students and one teacher at their high school in Columbine, Colorado.

The impact of the massacre—proliferated by nascent and hungry twenty-four-hour cable news channels—generated an urgent need to assign blame, not only for the sake of the families in Columbine but to soothe a shocked populace. Harris and Klebold were dead by their own hands, the black boxes of their minds forever sealed. Someone or something knowable had to be held accountable and so politicians, activists, and scientists began to analyze every facet of the tragedy in order to establish who to hold responsible and how to keep the rest of our children safe. Rap music, goth culture, and bullying were all proffered as potential scapegoats, but none attracted researchers and enraged citizens alike quite like videogames.[46]

One of the most thorny aspects of research culture in any field, and certainly the social sciences, is the way we like to espouse the sense that our work is driven by objectivity. However, strong cultural attitudes inevitably influence how we approach subjects for study, how we decide which projects receive funding and which manuscripts are favored for publication. For over a decade following Columbine there was a vested international interest—and a sudden influx of grant money from privately funded, now defunct organizations with dubious names like the National Institute on Media and the Family and the Center for Successful Parenting—in proving that videogames were dangerous.

Experimental psychologists played an especially integral, even zealous role in promoting this view. The reason, in part, was practical: Games were the least researched of the subjects that received scrutiny post-Columbine and therefore provided the greatest scope for quickly designed, novel studies that could be fast-tracked to publication. Before 1999, precisely zero psychological research articles on the relationship between violence and videogames had been published (only a few dozen mentioned videogames at all and most of them focused on exploring their cognitive and educational benefits). Since 1999, nearly two hundred such articles have been made readily accessible in the American Psychological Association's (APA) database.*

The other motivator for such targeted psychological research was, appropriately enough, psychological in nature. The scientists involved felt tremendous pressure to ease public anxieties and explain how "good kids" (that is, white and middle-class) could commit horrific acts. Games—unlike anger, sexuality, parenting, and mental illness—are tangible, which means they are removable; if games could be shown to be unilaterally harmful,

---

* This data was obtained by querying titles and abstracts in the APA's PsycNET database (psycnet.apa.org), which consists of nearly four million peer-reviewed research papers, using the term "videogames" (including variant spellings) combined with terms related to violence ("violence," "violent," and "aggression").

we could easily excise them from society.* But in trying to prove that games were corruptive, the researchers corrupted their methods. Marginal findings were paired with sweeping conclusions; concepts like violence and aggression were poorly defined and measured, leaving data open for egregious misinterpretation. At the same time, preeminent academic journals overlooked these obvious methodological problems and published the work anyway, as videogames were a hot topic.

To make an example of one 2005 study: Participants were tasked to play the first-person shooter *Doom* (a twelve-year-old title at the time of the study's publication, making it akin to an archaeological relic in videogaming's brief history).[47] Those assigned to the "violent group" were paired off and played the game more or less as usual, using guns to shoot pixelated demons, while those in the "nonviolent group" played a modified version in which they walked the game's lo-fi corridors with no weapons and nothing to do but work their way through the maze of each level ("boredom group" would have been a more appropriate designation). After twenty-five minutes of play, everyone was transitioned out of the game and into another computer program: a decision-matrix scenario, commonly used in social science research, in which participants had to choose to either cooperate with or defect from the other member of their pair to earn points. In effect, the researchers were testing how playing one outdated game affected the way people played a different, even less interesting game.

The study authors found that both groups were just as likely to act cooperatively and view the other person as trustworthy.

---

* Easily, at least, in fantasy. In reality, human beings don't have a great track record of taking things known to do more harm than good—cigarettes, say, or nuclear weapons—out of circulation.

However, they reported that the violent group was moderately more likely to defect than its counterpart. From this minor finding amid a plethora of statistically nonsignificant results, the authors concluded that "playing violent videogames may undermine prosocial and altruistic motivation . . . [and] appears to have contributed directly to participants' willingness to exploit. . . ."[48] Their interpretation—that cheating another player out of abstract points should be construed as antisocial and exploitative—was, to put it mildly, a stretch. It also ignored plausible alternative explanations, such as the idea that the so-called violent group, having spent the previous half-hour in the potential space of *Doom*'s action-horror world, was more primed than the group who spent the same amount of time bored out of their minds to view the decision-matrix game as another opportunity to play around with different ways of being in a safe space. In other words, members of the violent group may have been more likely to be exploitative because they were more innately aware that no one was actually being exploited. The study authors assumed that *Doom* had caused the "violent" participants to confuse the virtual world with the real world, when actually those individuals may have accurately assessed that both of the study's tasks took place firmly in the virtual world.*

Perhaps most significantly, this study that yielded little and yet labeled its findings "remarkable" was not published in an obscure academic journal desperate for submissions, but appeared

---

* It is worth noting that the study was not presented as wholly detached from real-world consequence. Participant pairs believed they were competing for a prize of a hundred dollars against all the other pairs in the study. The authors referred to the promise of this reward as generating a "high-stakes" situation, though they did not provide evidence of having assessed the degree to which participants—who were largely white, male university students—regarded it as such.

in *Psychological Science,* one of the most influential and widely distributed psychology journals in the world.[49] Its publication represented a total system failure along every check and balance of what was supposed to be the unbiased apparatus we call the scientific method.

An insular feedback loop ensued. The newly established body of gaming research literature, despite its limitations, was collectively cited by the APA in a 2005 resolution declaring that games had conclusively been shown to be harmful.[50] The resolution, in turn, prompted the APA to declare that its funding support for videogame research would now exclusively focus on intervention studies that took negative effects of gaming as a given and centered on determining how best to mediate those effects. Anyone seeking to challenge the status quo through scientific research was told in no uncertain terms to move on.

As the years progressed and anti-gaming research lost its cachet, it became obvious among those still paying attention how profoundly social science had failed in its mission of objectivity, succumbed to political pressures, and ultimately taught us little about the relationship between videogames and human behavior. Meta-analyses of videogame research literature—which combined data from individual studies in order to reveal broader trends—showed that no meaningful links between playing games and doing bad things in the real world had been established.[51] Unfortunately, this evidence emerged before a scientific community that had largely lost interest, the polemic fires that generated money and press having cooled. In 2013 an international group of 228 psychologists officially protested the APA's 2005 resolution, decrying it as premature and founded on weak, inconclusive evidence.[52] As if to drive home the point that the tides of public interest had long since departed, the APA spent two years taking this denouncement "under advisement" before releasing a revised resolution in 2015 that read like a copy-and-paste job of the original.[53]

Consequently, we are left with a decades-long stigma that, despite being rendered invalid, remains unchallenged. As recently as August 2019, following back-to-back mass shootings in El Paso, Texas, and Dayton, Ohio, President Trump and others specifically pointed the finger at videogames despite there being no factual reason to do so, while omitting critiques of more obviously relevant issues like xenophobia and access to guns.[54] Such blatant scapegoating has persisted unchecked because, while games are not dangerous in the way some people have feared since their inception, we lack a compelling alternative explanation. Absence of evidence is not a theory unto itself; we still need to address the concerns of the parent watching her child watching a screen. We still need to address the problems that we know exist from our own experiences and observations: that it is possible to feel like a game has gotten under our skin; to feel so angry at a game that we want to smash the controller into pieces—perhaps we have even done so.

So, if the game isn't making us feel or act in these ways, then what's going on?

THE FIRST TIME I met Cole he told me that he loved videogames, but also feared that they were bad for him. He was a bright young man in his senior year of college, preparing to begin a career in the tech industry. He sought me out for psychotherapy in anticipation of imminent life changes as he moved from school to autonomous adult life. Cole denied experiencing any acute problems at the time of our meeting, but he recalled, almost with nostalgia, how severe anxiety had been a part of his life since childhood, when he was beset by frequent and intense nightmares and a social reservation that made making friends difficult. Major transitions, he said, were particularly overwhelming and short-term psychotherapy at the start of high school and college had helped to ease him into those new phases of life.

Cole played games often, preferring competitive titles that he could practice alone and then play locally* with others. Despite his obvious fondness for playing and his awareness that I wrote about and often worked with people who played games, I noted a familiar embarrassment in Cole as he described this aspect of his life. He said that after a gaming session he tended to berate himself for not spending his time on "better things." Cole spoke about himself as though he were a post-Columbine stereotype, a "good kid" consumed by games and numbed to the outside world, and yet to me it seemed that image couldn't be further from the truth. He was, by his own report, a passionate guitarist and computer programmer; he had a solid group of close friends and a fulfilling romantic relationship; he received good grades at school and had an exciting job lined up for after graduation. What "better things," in his mind, was he not doing?

"I don't know," he said, shrugging casually. "But games can be addictive and I don't want to fall into that."

I worked with Cole several years after Jack but, in a pattern reminiscent of my treatment with Jack, Cole and I barely spoke

---

* Local multiplayer is a feature of games to be contrasted with online multiplayer: with the former, two or more players are physically in the same space, looking at the same screen on which both their characters are represented. Online multiplayer gaming requires no shared physicality: players coexist in game-space virtually, over the internet.

of games for the first couple of months of treatment. This time it was not out of my discomfort but because—despite his initial expression of concern over his gaming habits—Cole had other, more pressing issues on his mind. As college graduation drew nearer, the familiar symptoms of insomnia and nightmares returned and absorbed much of our attention. Cole was not alarmed by these experiences, however; I was again struck by how he spoke of them like old friends. "I really thought I had this stuff beat," he would say, before adding with a half-smile: "Guess not."

Our exploration of both his waking and dream life felt shallow to me; I found myself with no thoughts about why Cole was going through this resurgence of anxiety beyond the vanilla notion that graduating college is stressful. Though his sleep habits eventually normalized, I couldn't shake the idea that we had put little more than a Band-Aid on the problem, if we'd accomplished anything at all. But he had successfully finished college and was looking forward to what was coming down the road—perhaps I was only looking for problems where there were none.

One morning Cole came to our session in distress. He looked tired and physically on edge, feverishly tapping his feet and wringing his hands. I knew that the day before had been the first day at his new job and expected that this would be the source of his concern. But no: Cole wanted to talk about *Super Smash Bros. Melee*. Part of a long-running Nintendo franchise, the game centered around multiplayer brawls between various famous characters from the veteran company's pantheon and was a dorm-room favorite for its fast pace and ease of play, as newcomers could have fun smashing buttons on the controller with little thought of strategy. It was also a popular entry in the competitive gaming circuit for its focus on player-versus-player combat and its depth of system (at higher levels of play, the unique benefits and vulnerabilities presented by each character must be carefully considered). Cole's relationship with the game fell somewhere in the middle: He had never competed in any official tournaments but described the group of friends he typically played with as dedicated and highly skilled.

Cole told me that he had started playing *Smash Bros.* the night before with the vague idea of practicing a tricky combination move for Kirby, the marshmallowy hero of various Nintendo games since 1992 and Cole's character of choice. After about an hour, aware of his growing fatigue, Cole said he wanted to stop playing—but couldn't. "The worst part," he told me, "was that I just kept getting more tired and more frustrated, so with every passing minute I knew I was further from accomplishing the move I set out to practice in the first place." He attributed this loop to the game's "control" over him, which he believed resulted from a combination of the game's intrinsic addictive potential and his own "weakness" to resist. The night ended with Cole, by his description, shaking with rage and muttering expletives coarsely under his breath—this behavior, in turn, apparently frightened his girlfriend when he eventually entered the bedroom. "She said she doesn't like to see me like that," he said.

It was clear to me that Cole had internalized the hysterical dogma that games had the power to make him do things he didn't want to do. For him, the game was a trap he fell into: *Smash Bros.* was to blame for being addictive and Cole was to blame for lacking the strong moral fiber that would allow him to defy its pull. At the same time, he expressed fear that the enraged self that emerged at the end of the night somehow represented who he "really was, deep down." As though the game summoned from within an antisocial monster that only concerted effort—and avoidance of the game—could keep locked inside.

Packaging his experience in this way left little room for exploration or attributing specific meaning to his behavior: The game was bad, Cole was bad, or—most likely in his view—both were bad. Even more, it was unclear what, if anything, could be done about the problem. Cole didn't conceptualize the issue as something to be overcome; in fact, in the course of describing his helplessness before the power of the game, I realized that his physical agitation had vanished and he now sat calmly on the couch.

In an effort to better understand what was happening I knew we had to move past the image of the player-game relationship as one of "doer" and "done to." I asked Cole to take a step back and consider what had been going on prior to this episode with the game. His mind immediately went to his first day at work, which he described with utmost sincerity as "perfect." His responsibilities were interesting and indicated that his new boss, whom Cole found warm and engaging, held a genuine respect for Cole's technical skill set. The office had a laid-back environment and was stocked with free snacks. A coworker, Cole mentioned offhandedly, suggested that the two of them should play *Smash Bros.* together sometime. I observed with amazement that the further Cole worked his way down this list of allegedly positive experiences, the more manifestly anxious he became, until he was nearly back to the level of agitation he had displayed at the start of the session.

I wondered aloud if the job seemed not only perfect, but too perfect.

"Of course," Cole replied. "I can only fuck it up from here."

He was struck by how deeply he believed this statement, though he had not consciously considered it until that moment. I began recalling the various times over the past few months when Cole spoke of his anxiety symptoms with an incongruous fondness. It was true, he realized, that he took a certain comfort in these long-standing emotional problems, as they helped mollify expectations. If he performed well despite insomnia, it was a notable accomplishment, but if he performed poorly no one, including himself, would be overly disappointed. Cole credited this framework—working to exceed low expectations rather than meet high ones—with being the source of his good grades and supportive interpersonal relationships. Indeed, he seemed to feel paradoxically indebted to his anxiety for every positive aspect of his life!

We turned our attention back to the game. Rather than *Smash Bros.* taking over Cole, perhaps there was a way to understand his loop as a compulsion that arose from within, rather than a malevolent force that seized him from without. On one level, Cole said, he wanted to "ride the high" of the day and affirm his competence through mastery of a complicated move within the game. I suggested another level that both competed and coexisted with the first. After an exceptionally promising day, Cole looked to the game as a means of reestablishing his particular version of reality, one in which he was hopelessly outmatched by his anxiety and therefore could not be expected to succeed. By practicing the sequence in *Smash Bros.* beyond the point of exhaustion, a part of him knew that, in an unmotivated and fatigued state, he would never achieve his goal, thus confirming his limitations. The fantasy that reaching this emotional low then brought forth his "real" self—an agitated, angry monster who scared the people around him—bore a cathartic relief, even as it disturbed him. If Cole were destined to destroy any semblance of a "perfect" life by virtue of who he was deep down, failure wouldn't really be his fault.

The reaction of his girlfriend only reinforced the fantasy: Because Cole so rarely expressed angry feelings, their sudden arrival had alarmed her, particularly as they stemmed from a game that she did not understand could be a reasonable source of such intense emotion. Cole felt reaffirmed in his long-standing idea that anxious and angry feelings (flip sides of the same coin, as anxiety is emotional energy directed at the self, while anger is the same energy directed outward) were unacceptable, which also meant that personal contentment and success would be forever out of reach. Only after this equilibrium was restored could Cole's internal pressure dissipate and he could go to sleep. This conceptualization of Cole's behavior allowed us to discard the stigma around games without denying that the way he used games, at specific times, could be troublesome—both to him and those close to him. Seen as a corrupting force, the game became a scary problem with no obvious solution (other than, perhaps, eliminating all games, which Cole was loath to do as they mostly served as an enjoyable pastime both alone and with friends). Viewing the game as a potential catalyst of the player's psychological dynamics, however, opened up myriad ways to understand and address problematic game-playing behavior. Cole and I could then use what we had learned about his relationship to games in order to identify broader patterns in his life.

Some months after our discussion of *Smash Bros.* Cole arrived at a session appearing down. His job, he said, was not challenging him in the ways he had hoped, and he had just been contacted by a recruiter from a major tech company who spoke of an exciting opportunity there. This sounded like good news to me: a chance to advance his promising career or at least evidence that he would have options should he choose to make a change down the road. But rather than make assumptions, I simply noted without comment that Cole seemed sad. His face broke out in a sudden smile—not the half-smile we had both come to recognize as a sign that he was seeking paradoxical relief in his symptoms, but something qualitatively different. A full, toothy grin.

"This is going to sound weird," Cole said. "But I think I miss feeling anxious." He had grown accustomed to making decisions based on whether he felt he could bear the anxiety of change and with that anxiety reduced he was met with a strange new sensation of agency. Whether to take or leave a job now felt like Cole's choice to make and the lightness of freedom intermingled with the weight of personal responsibility. He added, with mock rage, "Dr. Kriss, what have you done to me?"

"Who, me?" I said. I was prepared to go on, to suggest that though I had played a role in Cole's recent psychological changes, he was ultimately the one in charge of his life. I would reinforce the notion that most relationships—whether between therapist and patient, parent and child, or player and game—cannot be reduced to something simple and one-sided, the doer and done to. But I didn't need to continue: Cole saw what I meant, what he was doing and started to laugh.

"I think I just tried to turn you into *Smash Bros.*," he said.

I nodded. "The old one, the one you felt had the power to control you. Things are looking different now. The game hasn't changed, exactly, but your position relative to it has."

"Yeah." For a split second, I thought I saw Cole instinctively twiddle his thumbs. "I guess I'm still figuring it out."

*

My work with Cole was illustrative of the internalized shame common in people who play games: Despite the fact that no factual link was ever established between games and deviant behavior, Cole had come to feel that his relationship with games meant that he was, somewhere inside of him, deviant. The collective knowledge that games exert a malevolent influence gave Cole a way to make sense of unpleasant emotional experiences like anxiety and anger when they arose in him. One reason he and I were able to challenge these old assumptions so effectively was that Cole's vision of himself as the stereotypical gamer kid so clearly defied reality: For the most part he lived a rich, multifaceted life, with no history of violence or other antisocial behavior.

It should not be considered a given that the same logic would apply to someone like Jack, who *would* become violent sometimes. In a sense, Jack bore all the signs of a mind that one might argue had been twisted by games: socially awkward and prone to aggressive outbursts directed at objects and, on occasion, his older brother. Many of the games he played were violent in the way the term had often been defined during the heyday of anti-videogame research: that is, they looked violent at a glance, featuring things like weapons, explosions, and the possibility of character death.*

---

* Little effort has been made in research to distinguish "violence" from "gratuitous violence" in games. Mainstream media discourse beginning in the early 2000s focused on legitimate grotesqueries from titles like *Grand Theft Auto 3*, in which the player's character could, for example, choose to pay for sex with a prostitute (the act of which was not depicted on-screen) and then murder her to retrieve the money he'd spent. But in an effort to hastily categorize all "violent" games as harmful, researchers (who knew little about the breadth and diversity of games to begin with) erroneously assumed that any title featuring a gun or a dead body would have the same impact on the psyche as a game like *GTA 3*, which explicitly sought to push the boundaries of social decorum. Such poor defining of terms encouraged the public to assume that all violent games were alike.

Was it beyond the realm of possibility that these games insidiously gave Jack the desire to act with violence in the real world?

Taken at its most literal, this premise seemed unlikely to me. An essential component to proving causality, according to the scientific method, is demonstrating that the thing thought to be the cause chronologically preceded the thing thought to be the effect. This would suggest that Jack's violent behavior in the real world would most likely occur shortly after playing a violent game, the latter triggering the former. (This was, after all, how many studies claiming to prove the relationship between games and violence were structured: Participants played a violent game, then immediately engaged in some task designed to measure their aggression or attitudes toward violence.) Based on Jack's accounts in our sessions, this was not the case. He almost exclusively played games late at night when the apartment was quiet. His behavioral outbursts most often occurred in late afternoon and early evening when everyone in the family was home and Jack's feelings of frustration were at their peak.

One notable exception to this pattern was an incident in which Griffin arrived home, drunk, in the early hours of the morning while Jack was playing *Mass Effect* in the living room. Griffin demanded Jack turn off the game so that he could watch a television program, inciting an argument that eventually escalated to a physical fight. Unlike many outbreaks of aggression when Jack said he was unsure why he acted the way he did, he expressed a clear understanding of this episode: He had felt his valued private time was under threat from his brother and thus felt impelled to defend it. Jack did not express a sense of having been keyed up for violence by the game, but rather the opposite: His sense of calm while playing was so thoroughly disturbed by

Griffin that Jack quickly became overwhelmed and resorted to a destructive (and unproductive, as Griffin won the fight and took over the TV) coping strategy.

Jack also never said, in describing a violent episode, that he was attempting to emulate something he'd experienced in a game. This raised another point: Assuming a direct cause-and-effect relationship between in-game and out-of-game violence implied that Jack's behavior in the world would mirror ideas with which the game had allegedly infected him. *Mass Effect*'s depiction of violence mostly involved squad-based melees in which Shepard and his crew faced off against various human and alien foes using futuristic weaponry and psychic abilities like telekinesis. Little in Jack's smashing of dinnerware or wrestling with Griffin resembled this. Even more, there was a striking emotional discrepancy between Jack's aggressive actions in the game—in which he felt competent and purposeful—and in his daily life, in which he felt helpless, impulsive, and believed that nothing he did got through to his family in the way he had intended. Jack's subjective experience of violence across the virtual and physical were so contrary that it was hard to conceive of how one could have possibly inspired the other.

ONE OF THE MOST glaring issues with the post-Columbine wave of violent videogame research was that scientists placed tremendous value on internal over external validity. Internal validity in research studies is achieved by isolating variables of interest and minimizing the impact of (i.e. "controlling for") other factors. Doing so comes at the expense of external validity, which is a measure of how much a study's results are directly applicable to how people function in the real world. The 2005 Doom study, for instance, had high internal validity: all participants were seen in the same physical environment (the authors' lab), played the same game (depending on random group assignment) for the same amount of time (twenty-five minutes), then took part in the same decision-making matrix. The only significant variable to change across participants was whether they played the "violent" version of the game or not, which meant that the authors could feel confident that any significant results they derived were due to differences along that single variable and nothing else.

The problem, of course, was that each step toward building such a tightly controlled laboratory study took the authors another step away from examining human behavior as it naturally occurs. Participants being instructed by a scientist to play a game for exactly twenty-five minutes (one version of which was not even the real game, but a modified "nonviolent" version of it) was not reflective of how people actually engage with games in real life. A computer-based decision-making matrix was also far from a realistic recreation of the kinds of social interactions and negotiations that most people typically encounter. So, while the study authors could say that the violent/nonviolent variable they manipulated was responsible for any fluctuations in the outcome variables they measured, they could not so easily claim that that translated into anything meaningful in understanding people's actual lives.

Studies that prioritize external validity are more immediately relatable to life as it exists outside of the laboratory, at the cost of being able to definitively say that variable x caused result y. Both internal and external validity studies are necessary to fully understand any psychological phenomenon, and external validity is particularly important when trying to draw conclusions about real-world social problems like violence. Few such studies exist in relation to videogames, but those that do have demonstrated a surprising finding that, when combined with internal validity studies, starts to paint a more nuanced picture of the relationship between games and violence.

Two epidemiological studies from 2011 used various statistical models to look for a relationship between people exposed to violent and nonviolent games and reported incidents of violent crime.[55, 56] Rather than trying to simulate violence in the laboratory—which demanded poor proxies like "defecting" in a decision-making game—these studies took documented violence in the world as its variable of interest. That game-playing was not shown to correlate with spikes in crime may by this point feel predictable, but even the studies' authors expressed surprise that data demonstrated that both violent and nonviolent game-playing were related to a *decrease* in violent crime.* When this idea is combined with the spate of internal validity studies that showed violent games increased (though often to small degrees) aggressive attitudes or actions within a laboratory setting, a theory more sophisticated and far more explanatory than "games cause violence" begins to emerge. For some, violent games serve as an outlet for aggressive feelings, which may in fact mitigate the impulse to act violently in the real world. The game is not a virus that infects the player with aggression, but rather an outlet for aggression already present in the player. Another way to put this is that the relationship between violent games and violence is closer to one of *displacement* rather than *imitation.*

---

* I say related because causation cannot be definitively established in external validity studies. Though the authors took pains to account for time-order—that is, charting that exposure to games *preceded* dips in crime rates—it was impossible for them to isolate all other variables that might have contributed to their findings, which is a necessary component in establishing cause-and-effect relationships.

Other external validity studies taking place on a more individual scale have supported this idea. The 2008 book *Grand Theft Childhood* detailed findings from a federally funded investigation into violence and videogames led by authors Lawrence Kutner and Cheryl K. Olson, who opted for a more phenomenological approach over epidemiological or laboratory-based methods. This meant that, rather than tracking relationships between variables, their data chiefly consisted of interviews with children, adolescents, and families. Their analyses represented an attempt to understand why people who already played violent games did so. They found that young players overwhelmingly cited reasons like, "It's something to do when bored," or, "I like to create my own world," when explaining their attraction to violent games.[57] Boys in particular said such games helped them to relax or "get anger out," though many girls endorsed those sentiments as well.[58] Players of titles like *Grand Theft Auto 3*—featuring highly violent systems and a realistic, modern setting—consistently showed an awareness that their in-game behavior would be frightening (and punishment-inducing), rather than fun, if translated into the real world.[59]

In some instances, Kutner and Olson suggested that a *lack* of game-playing could be a sign of social dysfunction and potential for violence, particularly in contexts where game-playing was considered normal.[60] It was widely assumed by media outlets and politicians that Seung-Hui Cho, the Virginia Polytechnic Institute student who killed thirty-two people with semi-automatic pistols on April 16, 2007 (nearly eight years to the day after Columbine), had been inspired by violent videogames. In fact, Cho didn't play games at all, which his roommates later said had contributed to their opinions of him as being strange and hard to relate to, since he repeatedly refused invitations to participate in their ubiquitous dorm-room pastime. Someone like Cho—socially isolated, insufficiently treated for serious mental illness—might have actually benefited from an outlet like videogames to expel his violent impulses, though games could never have taken the place of adequate gun control and mental health resources in averting the tragedy Cho perpetrated.*

Which brings us back to Jack: based on the perspective of games as an outlet for displaced aggression, Jack's occasional violent behavior was not caused by games but instead indicated that games were not always a sufficient coping mechanism to temper his impulses. Recall the events of Gamergate: Games didn't "make" anyone abuse or harass anyone else (their targets, after all, also played games). Like Jack resorting to an ill-conceived scrap with his physically stronger brother, Gamergate adherents chose to engage in real-world antisocial behavior because they had come to rely on games as their sole source of catharsis and did not know how to cope with their perception that this respite was being taken away.

As Jack and I would discuss (and as I will detail in Chapter 7), playing games often helped him to feel in greater control of his emotions and, by extension, his body. In moments of intense distress, however, he fell into the more instantly gratifying and

---

* If one's interest is to eliminate mass shootings, the problem starts and stops with gun control from a policy standpoint. Violence among mentally ill populations is quite rare and for the most part no more likely than in the general population.[61] Improving access to and quality of mental health treatment should be a priority in any society, but blaming mental illness for mass violence is choosing a scapegoat just like videogames. Better and more plentiful mental health resources do tangibly save lives, however, in the form of reducing suicide rates (though gun control makes a tremendous difference in this area, as well).

destructive desire to break things or fight. Games represented an alternative to violence, a more sophisticated way of dealing with stress. That it was not always effective was an important point to work on in therapy: we wanted to provide Jack with *more* resources like games, not take those resources away from him or decry them erroneously as the cause of his problems.

Viewing games as digital corruptors that make people act a certain way only serves to inhibit an appreciation of how Jack and others engage with games to explore diverse aspects of their natures—not all of which are necessarily socially attractive or mainstream. The long-standing and unscientific bias against games has muddied the waters of understanding beyond the debate over whether they cause violence. It has also trickled into the contentious and confusing issue of how to define and treat games addiction.

Chapter 6

Addiction

How should we understand and treat videogame addictions?

Do we always, always to the point of misery, do a thing?

—Saul Bellow, *Mr. Sammler's Planet*

Liz played *Candy Crush Saga*. A lot.

Its grip was insidious: At first, she barely noticed that tapping and swiping at the colorful match-three iPhone game had largely replaced the time she used to reserve for sleep. While playing she would absent-mindedly pluck at hairs on the back of her head; she started worrying that she was giving herself a bald spot. But Liz kept playing. "I can't help it," she told me during one of our sessions. "I'm addicted."

Liz was a person of many contradictions. At fifty, she alternately expressed feeling like "a kid who never grew up" and "a decrepit old woman." She worked sporadically as a temp while harboring a passion for acting, though she rarely went for auditions. Single and with virtually no history of romantic involvement, Liz would sometimes blame herself for being "undesirable," while at other times she derided the world for being filled with hateful, petulant men. Across these areas of life, her sense of self-worth and efficacy fluctuated wildly, and often, even during a single psychotherapy session, between self-loathing and grandiosity. A lifetime of feeling vulnerable to the quixotic whims of an uncaring world had led to a series of internal, unconscious compromises that, while born out of an instinct for self-protection, now left Liz deeply narcissistic in the Winnicottian sense. She refused to accept that the outside world did not always, in some way, connect back to her fantasies.

When Liz was younger this took the form of interpreting every interaction with a man as a sexual advance, every conversation with a woman as charged with envy. Now in middle age the interpretations had shifted, but the themes were unchanged. Whenever Liz rode the city's subway train and saw young people looking at their phones (so, in other words, every time she was on the train), she told me with utmost conviction that she "knew" they were secretly taking photos of her to show their friends later, in order to "share a laugh about this sad, disgusting old woman." If she could no longer conceptualize herself as the most beautiful, she must surely be the ugliest—either was preferable to the idea that she fell somewhere in the middle, and that most people around were simply indifferent to her.

Suffice it to say, Liz felt lost, angry, anxious, and frequently depressed—one would think *Candy Crush* would be the least of her problems. But about six months into our treatment the game started overshadowing all other topics of discussion. It began as the reason why Liz "couldn't think" during sessions. "I'm sorry, but I doubt I'll be able to focus on much of anything today," she would begin. "I was up all night playing on my phone, so now I'm just really . . . blah."

In the preceding weeks Liz had been making some small but significant changes in her life, such as going on more auditions and starting to create (but not quite finalizing) an online dating profile. Our relationship had also grown in trust and closeness and consequently we had begun circling around increasingly sensitive material regarding Liz's traumatic past and the role such experiences played in perpetuating her turbulent present. I suggested that not sleeping the night before our sessions was a means of slowing us down and subverting the positive changes happening in her life. She was quick to refute this interpretation: "It's not just the night before we meet, it's every night. And it's not me, it's the game."

Demographically speaking, *Candy Crush* was not an unusual selection for Liz. One study from 2017 suggested that when it came to an action role-playing game like *Mass Effect*, only 20 percent of total players are likely to be women, while the player base for a match-three game like *Candy Crush* is nearly 70 percent female.[62] One might postulate a number of reasons why Liz, who had never previously had an interest in videogames, would find this title accessible: *Candy Crush* was easy to play via her smartphone, requiring no specialized gaming equipment; its presentation of candies in a grid was free of violent or sexist imagery. But when I expressed interest in why this game, in particular, was so compelling for her, Liz shrugged. She said that she didn't think *Candy Crush* was anything special, just "a way to waste time." As though doing me a favor, she listed off some of the "obvious" reasons the game appealed to her: the "order and tidiness" inherent in a system predicated on matching and clearing grids brought her a sense of satisfaction, and the occasional experience of clearing many tiles at a time made Liz feel "productive." The game, she reasoned, served as a counterbalance to her disorganized and depressing life, a retreat into a world of recognizable shapes and vibrant colors. Many people who played *Candy Crush* might be expected to give a version of this assessment, which did not make it any less true for Liz. But I wondered what the game might mean to her on a more idiosyncratic level that could help us understand why she felt unable to stop playing.

As I pressed the matter, Liz's thinly veiled attempts to humor me gave way to open hostility. She resented my efforts to draw out some personal, psychological meaning from what she regarded as meaningless behavior. "'I feel like you don't believe me that I'm addicted," she said. "Would you ask an alcoholic why he likes gin more than bourbon? Addiction is addiction, isn't it?"

We don't need a diagnostic manual to confirm what many of us have experienced firsthand: the sensation of being hooked on a game. Perhaps we have, on one or more occasions, forced ourselves to delete a game from our phone or computer out of a concern that it was sucking up too much of our time. In more extreme cases, people may seek out treatment (whether self-propelled or at the insistence of loved ones) to address their experience of being addicted to a videogame. These people feel burdened by the game yet powerless to give it up. The question is not whether their pain is real, but how to understand it.

We may not need a diagnostic manual, but we've got one. The eleventh edition of the *International Classification of Diseases (ICD-11)*, published by the World Health Organization (WHO) in 2018 and widely used across countries and continents, featured a new entry called "gaming disorder." Symptoms of this condition include "impaired control over gaming (e.g., onset, frequency, intensity, duration, termination, context)," "increasing priority given to gaming," and "continuation or escalation of gaming despite the occurrence of negative consequences."[63]

Five years earlier the newest edition of the American Psychiatric Association's diagnostic manual, the *Diagnostic and Statistical Manual of Mental Disorders (DSM-5)*, proffered "Internet Gaming Disorder" as "a condition warranting more clinical research and experience before it might be considered for inclusion in the main book as a formal disorder."[64] This was a dressed-up way of saying that while the APA recognized a public and professional concern about games addiction, few social scientists had actually bothered to look into it yet. In the time between the publication of the *DSM-5* and the *ICD-11*, public demand for formal classification vastly outpaced the publication of relevant research. Spates of deaths in the 2010s linked to reports of people staying up for days at a time playing games, particularly in Asian countries like Taiwan and South Korea, set national governments on edge. The proliferation of smartphones was followed by an outpouring of public and private money directed toward the emerging problem (or perceived problem) of technology addiction. These developments resulted in innumerable founts of anecdotal wisdom and condemnation in the form of online opinion pieces and hastily written books. It was only a matter of time before the mental health community joined the fray.

In 2016, two years before the *ICD-11*'s release, a group of thirty scientists and scholars drafted a paper arguing that a separate games addiction diagnosis would be premature and unhelpful to both the public perception of people who play games and the treatment of game-related issues.[65] In a distressing case of history repeating itself, the group's grievances were eerily familiar to those that surrounded violent game research nearly two decades earlier: namely, they argued that the new diagnosis was rooted in poorly designed studies, and too few of them, rushed to publication in a climate of political fervor. Recent years had already seen a titanic rise in private clinics across Asia, Europe, and the United States claiming—without any evidence base or specific credentialing—to specialize in the new phenomenon of games addiction. By formalizing a diagnosis the WHO was only perpetuating a myth of scientific consensus where there was none. In truth, we do not agree on what the disorder is—or even *if* it is—let alone how best to treat it, which is the point of diagnoses in the first place.

Addiction theory is centered around the idea that, while people vary in vulnerability depending on heredity and life experience, the addictive property lies within the thing itself. This is a compelling notion for substances like alcohol, nicotine, or cocaine that chemically influence the brain to motivate future use. But games function differently. They are not substances one ingests and therefore cannot exert immediate and consistent effects on the brain. From a chemical standpoint, something like cocaine is exceedingly simple: It has an inviolate formula ($C_{17}H_{21}NO_4$) and within seconds of being taken imposes an inviolate neurological effect (inhibiting re-uptake of dopamine, serotonin, and norepinephrine in the brain), which translates into an inviolate bodily experience (increased autonomic response, such as rapid heart rate and increased body temperature) and subjective feeling (a euphoric rush). This sequence occurs no matter who you are, where you're from, or what your personality is like. Who becomes addicted is more complicated, requiring consideration of genetics and psychology, but the *addiction potential* lies primarily within the substance. Drugs like cocaine, nicotine, and opiate derivatives, for instance, are considered to have extremely high addiction potentials due to their fast, powerful, and uniform effects on the brain. Marijuana, by contrast, is considered less potentially addictive, as its effects on the brain tend to be more variable (while some users experience a relaxed high, others feel anxious and paranoid, and the same individual can have different experiences when using at different times).

Even games most commonly identified as "addictive" are too multifaceted to work like drugs with high addiction potential. *Candy Crush* is one such title: It unapologetically tries to draw the player in with mesmerizing graphics, a simple system based on moving pieces to make matches, and the promise of cathartic release upon clearing the grid. Liz clearly experienced that cycle of frustration and reward while playing. Yet countless others have downloaded the game, tried out the first level, declared "this is stupid" and deleted it without a second thought. The game is not a chemical—its allure is more sophisticated and seductive—and therefore the subjective experience of playing it cannot be universal.

We do label plenty of things as addictive that are not substances, of course. Gambling is one such construct long featured in psychiatric manuals. The argument is flimsier than with drugs, but it is still feasible to place the burden of addictive potential on the thing itself: gambling promises material reward (money) which, while less uniformly compelling than a chemical substance, has such a broad appeal that we might say the act of winning would excite almost anybody. Gambling activities are also designed with the explicit purpose of keeping the gambler involved, as his hope of winning big translates, most of the time, into paying more to whoever's running the show.

It's arguable that games like *Candy Crush,* which is free to download but fueled by an economy of microtransactions (in which players are regularly solicited to pay small sums of money in order to gain advantages, skip levels, or bypass in-game restrictions) are designed to hook people as much as any casino slot machine. But people also become fixated on games that have no such intention baked into their designs. After my brother and I purchased *Tetris* for our Game Boy, Nintendo did not gain any additional payments whether we played for one hour or one thousand, and at no point were we promised any reward at all apart from mastery of the game itself. After extended use, the Nintendo Wii console famously automatically paused to ask players, "Why not take a break?," suggesting its developers were interested in preventing, not promoting, behavior that might be construed as addiction. And Liz, for her part, never spent a penny on *Candy Crush* despite playing for hundreds of hours; if King, the game's developer and publisher, intended to draw someone like Liz in as a means to then pump her for cash, it failed spectacularly.

The chief limitation to understanding games addiction is, in my view, our use of the word "addiction." It immediately frames videogames as a kind of infection, which is precisely the incendiary notion that has failed to hold water in the years since Columbine. Games addiction is more accurately described as *compulsive play:* It is not the game that won't release the individual from its clutches, but the individual who cannot bring herself to leave the game. If the overwhelming drive to play can be understood and brought into consciousness then the individual becomes free to realize that she is not beholden to an "addictive" game like a puppet on a string, but is in fact in control of and responsible for herself and her behavior and is therefore free to change.

This does not absolve the game (and its developer) of all responsibility, but it does place greater responsibility on the player than a more traditional model of addiction. Recall that the player and the game are in a kind of relationship, and relationships run the gamut from healthy to toxic, supportive to abusive. Relationships are a fundamental unit of human existence, things we instinctively pursue for survival and fulfillment, and as such they have the capacity to occupy as many roles in life as there are spaces to fill them. Good psychotherapy returns regularly to questions of relationships: How does the patient connect with herself and others, including the therapist? What does the patient bring to every relationship and what emerges uniquely when she and a specific other (human or computer) are together in the same space (physical or virtual)? A relationship can breed toxicity by reenacting old abuses, which serves to validate the patient's belief that nothing better can be expected—a belief she was forced to learn (and then forgot she learned) earlier in life when she was powerless to seek safety elsewhere. A relationship can also be healing, demonstrating to the patient that a level of understanding and acceptance previously thought impossible is, in fact, available to her. Relationships sustain us, tantalize us, drive us to impulse and self-destruction, and motivate us toward improvement and self-reflection.

Games addiction or, rather, compulsive play, is a window into the dysfunctional relationships from which we struggle to break free. By understanding those relationships and our participation in them we better understand ourselves.

✳

"*ADDICTION IS ADDICTION*, isn't it?" Liz was adhering to a self-limiting point of view, even if she didn't know it: In her mind, the game had seized her and would not let go. From this vantage Liz could easily dismiss any deeper meaning behind her compulsive play.

We could have left it there and turned our attention to practical methods of weaning Liz off the game, just as one might in a treatment focused on smoking cessation. But I didn't think that would provide any long-term relief. The arrival of *Candy-Crush*-as-symptom came too close to her recent progress to be coincidence; removing the game from Liz's life would surely only lead her to find another way to express the conflict inherent in her compulsion. Furthermore, Liz wasn't explicitly asking that we work to reduce her time playing the game. She simply presented it as evidence for why she couldn't fully participate in the therapy process and to direct my attention to her hair-pulling habit, which she did say she wanted to stop. There was little benefit in my trying to force the matter; Liz had made it abundantly clear that she was not interested in looking at her game-playing that way. So, I waited. If, as I suspected, *Candy Crush* had greater significance than being "a waste of time," if Liz was in a relationship with it and not just using it like a drug, the truth would eventually come out.

One day, Liz began the session: "I went to this workshop yesterday. The woman who gave the workshop was a casting director and, I don't know, I really liked her. She was warm and really knew about acting, not like some of the people they bring in for these things who claim to 'know the business' but are really secretaries. And afterwards everyone was going up to this woman and saying, 'Can I give you my headshot, blah, blah, blah.' So, I waited and then went up and said something like, I don't know, that I really appreciated her and what she had to say. And then the next day I emailed her, I guess it was the opportunist in me." Liz pulled out her phone and began to search through it before continuing. "And she sent me back this reply . . . and I know I can be sensitive and I guess read into things, but her reply made me think that she got the impression that I've had a lot of bad experiences with casting directors."

"Haven't you?" I asked. "Haven't most actors?"

"Yeah," she said, "but . . . it still bothered me!"

"Did you have some fantasy of what you wanted her reply to be?"

"I guess 'Thank you,' which she did say and, I don't know. 'Can you come in Tuesday for an audition?'" She let out a heavy sigh. "The way she said it here, she said, 'Here's hoping for happier auditions.' It just . . . like she assumed I'm not doing very well. Can I read you the full email?"

I attempted to shift us from the message on Liz's phone and toward the emotion swirling, unnamed, in her sigh. "You felt loving feelings for this woman," I ventured.

"I did! I really, really liked her. She was warm and I guess, can you say 'earthy' . . . ?"

"And you wanted her to return that love to you. Anything less than that was going to feel like a disappointment."

Liz paused. "It's funny, I think part of why I liked her so much is that I kind of transmogrified her in my mind to look like my sister . . . back when she and I got along, that is. Is that crazy?"

"Not at all," I said. "Transmogrification is one of the main jobs of the unconscious."

We both laughed lightly, then fell into a long and palpably melancholy silence.

"I used to admire my sister so much," Liz said. "Look up to her."

"When was that?"

"A long time ago."

Another pause, and she stared at her phone, which she had continued to hold in her hand throughout our discussion. Suddenly, Liz's demeanor changed, as though she were trying to rouse herself out of her current sadness. "I actually almost called my sister last night, because I couldn't figure out this goddamn level in *Candy Crush*."

This was the first time the game had emerged as part of a spontaneous train of thought, rather than a deliberate topic Liz evoked to justify her tiredness or disinterest during a session. She went on, also for the first time, to describe an aspect of her unique relationship with *Candy Crush*, in the form of a gripe: Despite having played the game for countless hours, she said she repeatedly found herself baffled by its "jelly levels." In these levels—the most common type in the game—some spaces on the virtual gameboard were encased in translucent jelly that needed to be removed through matching candy pieces on those spaces. Essentially, jelly added one additional step to clearing a grid and completing a level; privately, I knew it was no more complex than that. Yet Liz seemed totally unable to grasp how the jelly system functioned or what actions caused it to be removed and, thus, allowed for forward progress.

"I'll spend a long time on these levels and sometimes I'll win and I don't know why," she said. "But mostly I just spin my wheels . . . I know I'm supposed to do something with these shells around the pieces, at least I think that's right. That's why I thought about calling up my sister, because I know she also plays the game. I figured I could ask her what the hell I'm supposed to do, but then I thought, how embarrassing is that?"

I knew from previous discussions that embarrassment—or more accurately shame—was a defining characteristic of Liz's relationship with her sister. They rarely spoke, and saw each other even less, despite living in the same city. Married and stably employed, her sister seemed to exist in Liz's mind solely to remind Liz of her chronic failures. That, of two children from the same parents, one grew up to be happy and the other miserable was in Liz's eyes incontrovertible evidence of a random universe within which she was a hapless peon, a sentiment she expressed through a repertoire of clichés: Liz often said that she had simply "drawn the short end of the stick" in life or been "born under a bad sign."

This session was the only occasion I'd heard Liz allude to past feelings of warmth or admiration toward her sister, a suggestion that her bitterness over years of bad luck might have begun as loving feelings that went unrequited (or were perceived by her as such). A similar cycle had played out the day before in microcosm with the casting director, onto whom Liz projected a vision of her sister: Liz felt a connection toward someone she viewed as admirable and wise, had reached out, and then inevitably interpreted the response—however kind or supportive it actually was—as a rejection. After all, what else could she possibly expect from the world? She was pitiable and old, had lived through too many bad experiences. It was too late for her.

Liz also lived out a version of this cycle night after night with *Candy Crush,* using the game as a means of perpetuating the view that she was a hopelessly outmatched woman in a cruel and unpredictable world. By unconsciously refusing to learn the basic rules of the game, she condemned herself to be forever struggling, bewildered, and stuck—while feeling simultaneously convinced that her sister experienced no such troubles. In the face of the increased self-efficacy and personal growth she had been experiencing in recent weeks (the fact that she even attended the casting director's workshop being evidence of this), a major conflict had developed, and *Candy Crush* was the field, or at least one of the fields, on which this battle was being waged. Would Liz discard the worldview she'd held on to for all these years—a worldview that neatly explained why success and contentment had eluded her without needing to take responsibility for her choices—in favor of a less depressed, more authentic life? Or would confronting this new reality be too painful, even if it meant staying mired in her old ways?

Liz described the frustration loop of *Candy Crush*, including its vexing jelly levels, as "oddly comfortable, in the sense that it makes me feel numb." At the same time, the hair-pulling she engaged in while playing caused a great deal of discomfort and distress. As a fifty-year-old woman who easily looked ten years younger, Liz seemed to be artificially trying to transform herself into her vision of a "decrepit old woman" by making herself bald, one hair at a time. This was the cost of sticking to her old ways. She could have the game, where her confusion was justified and the rules made no sense and she could spend hours (or years) numbly going nowhere . . . but that would mean that a vital part of her was dying, plucked away, bit by bit, like so many black hairs.

The rapport Liz and I had built over the previous months allowed this metaphorical interpretation of *Candy Crush*—which recast her addiction as a form of compulsive play—to be discussed openly. She was skeptical at first.

"It's just a game," she said. "I don't know that it's fair to read so much into it."

"Fair?" I repeated. "Who decides what's fair?"

"I mean you talk about the unconscious and how playing the game is repeating an old pattern. I understand that, or some part of me does. But I don't know if I agree. The fact is I've always been a weak person . . ."

"You've felt weak, maybe for a long time. Maybe as long as you can remember. But that's a feeling, not a fact."

Liz laughed in a sharp, guttural voice laced with bitterness. "Jesus Christ. What are you saying? I've been wrong about myself all this time?"

"You present the idea that you're too weak to stop playing *Candy Crush* as an immutable fact. All I'm saying, in this moment, is: 'Says who?'"

She paused, her body and face seemed to contract. "Something is making me very angry," she said quietly. Her ability to name this emotion rather than suppress it, project it onto me or otherwise deny its presence was, in and of itself, a sign of Liz's progress in therapy.

"I think it's upsetting to hear that you have a choice," I said.

Her face turned red, she raised her hands and she cried out to the ceiling, "Yes!"

It was a strange catharsis, somewhere between rage and ecstasy. We sat in silence for a moment and I could see the release of tension was beginning to re-form as coherent thought in Liz's mind. She spoke quietly, still looking at the ceiling. "I've been depressed for almost forty years. I can't stop now. I can't."

"Why?"

Liz wasn't crying, but there was an atypical mistiness about her, as though a small amount of pressure from an ancient dam had been released.

"Sometimes when I'm in bed late at night," she said, "I imagine I'm in prison. It's dark, and my only cellmate is this awful, snarling dog. Or he's like a guard dog, guarding the exit, making sure I don't even dare get out of bed. This sounds crazy . . . I've never said it out loud before. And I've never quite connected, that playing the game and pulling out my hair . . . when I do those things I stop having those thoughts." She met my eyes. "My whole life I've been in prison—sorry, I've *felt* like a prisoner. You're saying the door's been unlocked the whole time. But if I leave now that means I could have left earlier but didn't. What a horrible thought!"

Liz was articulating one of the hardest aspects of change, in or out of psychotherapy. To see oneself as free to choose a different path is to confront the idea that the current path, however miserable, has also been a choice. An unconscious choice, most likely: for Liz, one made decades earlier, as a child trying to figure out why the world seemed so cruel and unpredictable, while her sister thrived and her parents acted as though the discrepancy between the two was due to Liz's innate deficits. This was what she clung to: A vision of the world that brought coherence to years of confusion and neglect. Letting it go meant letting go of Liz's unconscious wish that she was destined to this life, "born under a bad sign," and acknowledging the painful truth that she was here, in therapy, depressed and enraged, because of choices her parents made and because of choices she made. It didn't have to be this way, but it was. Now it was a matter of deciding whether she wanted to commit to the fantasy of fate or open up the possibility of shifting forty years of misery toward something different.

"Is the thought so horrible," I asked, "that it's worth staying in prison to avoid thinking it?"

LIZ AND I NEVER HAD TO ENACT specific strategies for kicking the *Candy Crush* habit. Once she became aware of the inner dynamics—the compulsion to recreate a specific narrative of her life—that had been driving her play, she couldn't help but think about them, if only for a split second, whenever she reached for her phone. Game-playing morphed from an affliction to a choice, which meant in turn that Liz had to take some measure of responsibility over the impact *Candy Crush*—and her other choices—had on her life. The path of change would not be instant or linear, but as a former supervisor once said to me: Once you glimpse the view from the mountaintop you never quite forget it, even if you descend, for a time, back into the valley.

In the end, Liz never deleted *Candy Crush* from her phone. She would tell me that she still found it a suitable diversion when riding the subway or waiting to be called into an audition. But it no longer held sway over her thoughts and sleep patterns; she no longer felt "addicted" to it. The goal was never for her to stop playing games, but to end the compulsive feeling that she *had* to play. The broad aim in any mental health treatment amounts to this: To establish a sense of internal freedom to live the life you want.

NOT EVERYONE IS, as Liz was, already in the midst of a psychotherapy treatment when the specter of compulsive play emerges. That scenario is, of course, far less common than one in which the behavior has developed and begun to cause problems and neither the individual nor his loved ones know where to turn or what to do about it. They may not even know how to think about it.

A couple of years ago a colleague contacted me requesting a little assistance. She was in the middle of a psychological assessment of a seven-year-old boy named Mickey, who was brought in by his mother after reports from school that Mickey was being "disruptive": talking out of turn, struggling to focus on in-class assignments, and at times seeming unable to physically stay in his seat for extended durations.

Unlike psychotherapy, assessment is a targeted process in which the answer to a single, pointed question (such as, "What is causing Mickey's disruptive behavior?") is sought through the administration of a battery of tests. My friend's approach was comprehensive: She assessed Mickey's cognition, memory, attention, executive functioning, and academic knowledge and, through tasks done with Mickey and questionnaires completed by his parents, attempted to gauge emotional factors like depression, anxiety, and the quality of relationships with family and friends.

The value of assessment lies in its speed and specificity: In the course of a handful of meetings over a couple of weeks, my friend would gain a robust perspective on Mickey's functioning and from there could make determinations and recommendations to address the question at hand. If the assessment suggested a neuropsychological issue like attention deficit/hyperactivity disorder (ADHD), for instance, referral to a psychiatrist for medication might be warranted; if Mickey's distractibility seemed rooted in emotional distress, child or family psychotherapy would be far more likely to help. If the assessment turned up no significant issues to merit immediate psychological or pharmacological intervention, my friend might sit down with Mickey and his parents to brainstorm ways of helping Mickey feel more engaged with his schoolwork or ways to better cope with the demands of the teacher who had originally identified Mickey as disruptive.

In addition to all this, however, my friend was concerned that another factor might be at work, one for which she had no instrument to measure: What if Mickey was having trouble at school because of videogames? The hypothesis hadn't emerged out of whole cloth. It had been suggested with some insistence by Mickey's mother, Rebekah, at the start of the assessment process. According to Rebekah, Mickey was addicted to *Minecraft*. They had tried everything, from time limits to carrot-and-stick negotiations to confiscating his computer entirely—all to no avail. He kept playing, at home or with friends and, when possible, at the computer lab at school. And now, Rebekah reasoned, the game's toxic influence had bled into the classroom.

My friend felt games were outside her expertise; she thought I might weigh in on the idea that a game could affect Mickey in the way his mother feared. The research literature, after all, was sparse and contradictory—even though my friend thought the idea unlikely, wasn't it at least possible? I agreed to meet with Mickey and Rebekah.

To CALL *MINECRAFT* A VIDEOGAME is akin to calling *Star Wars* a movie: While technically accurate, the descriptor fails to capture how the work has achieved the status of cultural phenomenon. First released to the public as an in-development project in 2009, the game was originally built by a single programmer in Sweden named Markus Persson. Without a publicity machine or conventional marketing, *Minecraft* became a virtual word-of-mouth sensation—it was a commercial and critical success before its final version was even released. Versions of *Minecraft* have since been made for nearly every digital platform in existence; an international convention devoted exclusively to the game sells out thousands of tickets within hours every year; boundless merchandise and media tie-ins proliferate, and in 2014 Microsoft purchased the game and the software development company that grew around it for $2.5 billion. *Minecraft's* unprecedented grassroots ascension speaks to the appeal of its system and its world. It began as a side project that Persson created while working a full-time job but flourished because he had stumbled onto something special, something we hadn't even realized we'd been missing.

Minecraft is best described as playing inside a vast, virtual sandpit. The player inhabits an unnamed human character through a first-person perspective and begins the game set down in a procedurally generated* world filled with various ecosystems—from forests to deserts to mountains to oceans. The look of the world is quaint: everything has a pixelated, low-resolution quality, as if drawn from an earlier generation of videogames when technology was too limited to make things appear vivid and realistic. But the blockiness is in fact a key part of *Minecraft's* unique system:

---

* Procedural generation in games is the use of mathematical algorithms to create virtual spaces. The game designer writes the basic rules for how a space is to be built (that forests tend to grow next to rivers, say, or that certain animals tend to travel in packs) but the computer actually constructs it. Because no human has to oversee every aspect, procedurally generated worlds can be far larger (and much more quickly created) than worlds hand-built by human beings. The 2016 space exploration game *No Man's Sky,* for instance, used procedural generation to construct a universe of over 18 quintillion planets, more than any person could ever hope to visit—let alone design—in a hundred lifetimes.

Everything in the world can be broken down into component parts, one cube at a time. Trees are made of many wood cubes stacked together, deserts a near-infinite series of sand cubes. Dig out some dirt cubes from the ground and you may eventually hit a bed of stone cubes—dig deeper and who knows what you'll find (as the name suggests, mining is a major aspect of the game and the chief way for players to obtain rarer and more valuable materials). Once players collect raw materials they can craft a dizzying array of objects with them. When starting a new game, one typical choice might be to gather some wood and rocks in order to craft a stone axe, which then makes wood chopping a lot easier. From there you can quickly accrue a large amount of wood to build yourself, block by block, a log cabin.

This is only the beginning. Players are free to do whatever they please as they continue to mine materials and craft objects from them. Some may choose to play architect on a vast citadel made of precious stones and metals, while others may build themselves a simple skiff and some fishing equipment before setting off on a life at sea. The game offers multiple modes: One compels the player to focus on safety and survival (dangerous creatures start roaming the world at night) while another, known as "creative mode," allows the player to explore and build without danger. Players in this mode have created everything from full-scale cities inspired by fantasy works like *Game of Thrones* or *The Lord of the Rings*, to meticulous recreations of real-world places like the Taj Mahal or the Acropolis, to more baffling feats like the construction of a working computer inside the game world.[66]

The draw of *Minecraft* is rooted in its offering near limitless choice to the player within the bounds of a highly simplified world. Anything can be constructed given enough time, patience and planning; even the grandest tower is built one cube at a time.* Perhaps equally important to the game's success is that anything can be shared. Whether through uploading photos or videos of your creations or allowing players from anywhere in the world to traverse your world by hosting it on a server; *Minecraft* is inherently aspirational. The possibilities within the game are so varied and vast that only by seeing what others have dared to attempt do you start to locate what you are capable of (and interested in) attempting.

WHEN I SAT DOWN for an interview with Mickey and his mother, he struck me as a fairly typical seven-year-old boy: friendly, curious, distractible when a subject didn't interest him and attentive when it did. I introduced myself as someone who was there to help with his assessment, but that instead of doing more tests we would all just talk for a bit. Mickey spoke genially about friends, more hesitantly about schoolwork. He frequently looked to his mother after speaking, as though seeking her approval of his words, and she would respond with a warm smile. Eventually I said, "I hear you like *Minecraft*."

He looked at his feet and replied in a sullen monotone: "I'm addicted to it." This sounded very much like something he had been told, perhaps even something he had come to anticipate that adults wanted to hear.

"And what does 'addicted' mean, do you think?" I asked.

"That my mom says I play too much."

I chuckled reflexively and he eyed me with suspicion. Here

---

* That particular distinction likely goes to a hundred-story interpretation of the Tower of Babel that one player constructed in 2012 out of seven million blocks.

was the shame I had come to recognize as all too familiar. Rebekah jumped in with an anxious intensity that contrasted with how patiently she had allowed Mickey to speak for himself until this point.

"It's all so foreign to me," she said. "I see him doing whatever he's doing in the game and all I can think is, 'How is he taking this all in?'"

It was immediately apparent to me that Rebekah genuinely wanted her son to be safe, happy, and healthy—the idea that her attitude toward *Minecraft* had likely contributed to Mickey's internalized sense of shame would be devastating. I empathized with her and said as much: The game was alien to her and so she instinctively feared it and the impact it might have on her child. The good news, I told her, was that the game did not have to remain so opaque.

I asked Rebekah why she thought Mickey liked *Minecraft* so much. She said that she often watched him play, vaguely on the lookout for objectionable material, but in truth not really knowing what to make of it all. I invited her to shift her point of view. Rather than parsing the game for red flags, I wondered if she and her son might together reflect on what Mickey generally enjoyed doing in this world known for being a virtual sandpit, where players could choose to build, explore, fight, farm, and so on as they saw fit.

She thought for a moment and said that, actually, it was interesting, because she'd noticed that lately her son and a few other boys who often played together had developed a very particular routine. They would all log on to a shared *Minecraft* server (technical jargon that she admitted made more sense to Mickey and his friends than to her) and, within virtual walking distance from one another, they would each build large, intricate structures out of the various materials that could be scavenged and forged within the game: wood, stone, steel, onyx.

Mickey joined in the conversation to describe this pastime. As a group, he and his friends would tour each other's creations, commenting by in-game chat, snapping screenshots for posterity and perhaps adding little touches—a window here, a torch-bearing sconce there. Finally, once a given feat of architecture had been adequately admired, the gang would gleefully work together in razing the whole thing to the ground. Mickey giggled in describing this, and Rebekah looked at him with a mixture of love and befuddlement. "He does get such a kick out of it," she said.

In having mother and son walk through the ritual in full—rather than dismissing it as "doing whatever they do" in the game—I could more easily make the argument to Rebekah that Mickey and his friends were engaging with *Minecraft* in a way that held meaning beyond the mindless grip of addiction. These children were clearly leveraging a shared virtual space toward play that was not only complex, but developmentally appropriate for their age: they were experimenting with creating and sharing, not to mention enduring the frustration of critique. In each iteration they toyed with the balance between the catharsis of destruction and the loss of something cherished, instinctively searching for a middle ground that was at times achievable, at other times elusive.

Mickey stepped out of the room to join my colleague for another task. I told Rebekah that I didn't think *Minecraft* was the source of her son's difficulties in school. I did, however, think the game was important to him and could be a source of valuable insight into her son's psychology. The reason people tend to spend a lot of time inside a virtual world is because doing so serves some purpose—understanding that purpose necessarily precedes any change in behavior. She thanked me, thoughtfully acknowledging both relief and disappointment that videogames weren't "the answer," and we parted ways.

Several months later, I received a phone call from Rebekah. We had not been in touch since our one meeting; I didn't even know the final results of Mickey's assessment, as I had only been brought on in a consulting capacity. Rebekah said the assessment had been very helpful—my colleague found no serious neuropsychological or emotional issues, but her tests had picked up a previously undiagnosed learning disorder. Mickey was mildly dyslexic and, in retrospect, it struck both his parents and teacher as obvious that the lessons and assignments related to reading were those most likely to prompt his disruptive behavior. Mickey was now receiving extra help in this area and seemed to be improving. But Rebekah said all that had nothing to do with why she was calling.

"I just felt I had to tell you about what's been going on here," she began. "It was probably a month after our meeting, it was the afternoon, Mickey had finished his homework and was having some computer time before dinner. Suddenly he ran into the kitchen, where I was, and he was crying, just completely hysterical. I almost never see him like that. And I asked him what was wrong." Apparently, Mickey and his friends had just finished tearing down one of Mickey's elaborate *Minecraft* palaces. After everyone had logged off, Mickey started reviewing the screenshots he had taken before the destruction had begun. To his horror, Mickey realized that he had neglected to snap a shot of what he told his mother was "the coolest room he'd ever built"—an underground swimming pool—and fell instantly into despair.

"Normally I would have said something like, 'It's OK, don't take these things so seriously,' and, on the inside, just been totally confused. Or, let's be honest, I probably would have said, 'See? This is why *Minecraft* is bad for you.' But I had been thinking a lot about what you and I had discussed. So, I told Mickey that I knew how much his buildings mean to him and that it's sad that he doesn't have all the pictures for this one that he would have liked. And we started talking about it and about what it means when something we care about is gone and how we remember things that are gone and I just couldn't believe all he had to say."

Rebekah told me that this event catalyzed a regular tradition of what she and Mickey called their "*Minecraft* talks," in which the two of them would sit down and discuss what Mickey had been doing in the game recently. She said that not only had this helped her understand the game and her son's relationship to it but that, since relating to Mickey in this way, she was finding it easier to place reasonable restrictions on his play. "Before I would just tell him 'no' or take the game away. He wouldn't know why or I'd say something that probably confused or frightened him, like, 'It's rotting your brain.'" She laughed. "Now, it's funny, I think he feels that I respect him more, so when I tell him it's time to stop it's more like, 'All right, Mom gets me, she must know what she's talking about.'"

WE CALL SOMETHING AN ADDICTION when we believe there is nothing else to understand: We do the thing because we can't not do the thing. For Liz, this conceptualization was self-imposed: She played to dissociate, to avoid thought, to unquestioningly repeat old patterns. For Mickey, addiction was imposed on him by his mother, who was well-intentioned but simply didn't know how else to categorize an activity that so many others regard with distrust. In both cases, once the burden of meaninglessness was lifted everyone found it easier to actually think about the relationship between player and game—to respect it, in Rebekah's words—and how that relationship fit into the player's broader life. Beyond the monolithic catch-all of "addiction" awaited understanding and change—in other words, health.

Chapter 7

Health

How can videogames help people to heal?

I certainly wasn't happy. Happiness has to do with reason, and only reason earns it. What I was given was the thing you can't earn, you can't keep, and often don't even recognize at the time; I mean joy.
—Ursula K. Le Guin, *The Left Hand of Darkness*

A criticism often levied at clinical psychologists, and sometimes rightly so, is that our training skews us to view the human experience through the lens of pathology. As the depressive, anxious, or psychotic aspects of a patient's life tend to be the focus of treatment, it can be easy for any therapist to regard these aspects as more important than those that do not produce symptoms. Patients, in turn, have a keen ability to sense this prioritization and internalize it in an effort to please: Not infrequently someone will come to my office bemoaning that she has "nothing interesting to say," as though it were her responsibility to entertain me rather than my responsibility to be curious about whatever is on her mind.

In other spaces the pressure to win the approval of others may look very different: being the good daughter could mean never expressing anger, while the good employee never says "No" when asked to work late. But in the therapy space the "good patient" is presumed to be one never in short supply of a juicy problem, a perplexing neurosis, a dream thickly laden with double entendre.* The patient and I may come to find that "nothing interesting to say" is actually code for her feeling excited or at peace—code, also, for the assumption that I would find such emotions irrelevant to our work. The truth is quite the opposite: Illness can only be understood in light of health.

As the only species in the world capable of comprehending how incomprehensible the world is, we tend to rely on extremes as a way to simplify or otherwise bring coherence to our lives. Ambiguity and uncertainty can be so frightening that, in an effort to distance ourselves from them, we make a bad situation worse. We fail at something and decide this one instance proves the rule, that we *always* fail; a loved one betrays our confidence and we generalize this to the entire population, that people can *never* be trusted. And sometimes we pursue visions of health that seem ideal but, in their extremity, are as destabilizing as illness: that is, we strive to be happy all the time.

Health is balance. No one is happy (or sad, or angry, or anxious) every minute of every day. Trying to hold on to a state of feeling indefinitely is an exercise in self-judgment and exhaustion, denying the basic physiological reality that our bodies naturally try to revert to a neutral baseline. Health is recognizing that we will never be rid of sadness, or anger, or anxiety, but also that they will never hang around forever. In that knowledge we can come to appreciate what so-called negative emotions have

---

* The ubiquity of this pressure once led journalist Janet Malcom to proclaim that the psychoanalytic patient's true goal was to embrace "the freedom to be uninteresting."[67]

to teach us: Sadness is not our enemy, it is as much a part of us as happiness. It is the therapist's job to remind both his patients and himself that life is about more than being unwell, and also that wellness is about more than feeling happy. This also holds true when thinking about games. Games, after all, are meant to be fun, challenging, and thought-provoking—to discuss them in relation to violence and addiction but not joy would be akin to writing a cookbook that instructs how to avoid being poisoned while neglecting to include a single recipe.

The nature of joy in games can be difficult to pin down, however, and it certainly has little to do with happiness. This can be one of the most inscrutable truths when a parent, partner, or friend watches a loved one playing. Why does she do it, they ask, when it seems to cause her so much frustration? What enjoyment can he possibly be drawing from staring, mouth agape, at a screen? As previously discussed, games are potential: the player may actively explore and develop parts of herself that for one reason or another feel harder to access in the physical world. The game's presentation of bounded freedom—autonomy within a limited system—aids in this effort through the reduction of ambiguity. Often, we feel stymied in decision-making because the uncertainty of the future seems too great and the consequences of our choices too weighty. Spontaneity and being present in the moment are disrupted by an anxiety that we may take the "wrong" path (which carries the presumption that there is an unambiguously "right" path) and that the world will not forgive our mistake. The liberation of freedom collides with the burden of responsibility and we feel paralyzed: unable to think, feel, or act; unable to experiment with what it means to be ourselves. Games, unbound as they are from the weight of the real world, can facilitate such experimentation. The result rarely looks like happiness but is frequently felt as joy.

Frustration yields to a sense of mastery; repetition brings feelings of comfort and control. One might turn to a given game to be challenged in some way, making success valuable only insomuch as failure seems likely: a player fumbles through the "Crazy Train" solo on *Guitar Hero*'s expert mode to push his dexterity; another ponders for hours over a puzzle in *Myst*, determined to think her way through it rather than look up the solution online; still another huddles nervously in front of *Silent Hill 2*, lights out and curtains drawn, as a kind of test of his emotional regulation—can he immerse himself in the game's dread without becoming overwhelmed by it? Triumphs also often go beyond the private victory of player over computer, as in a game like *Fortnite* where success means surviving a battle royal against up to a hundred other players until there is only one left standing.

Someone else (or that same person, with a different game) may alternately play not to engage in competition but as a means to self-soothe, finding a sense of safety and calm in methodical exploration and repetitive actions. One player responds to a title's audio-visual aesthetic while another is engrossed in its depictions of character and setting. A third person may have little interest in style or story but finds the system of the game to be thrilling. Countless others relate to the game through some combination of all these factors, and more. As with other phenomena we have seen, the fun of videogames is rooted in the unique relationship that forms between the player and the game, a relationship that at its best helps the player relate more fully to himself.

The player knows this—though often not consciously—and so his play can be regarded as part of the innate human instinct toward health. It is this same instinct that often brings someone to psychotherapy despite not fully knowing why he has come—someone like Jack, for instance. Through all the chaos, the traumatic past events, the current pull from his family to accept dysfunction as normality, a part of him—when he sat in front of me and when he sat in front of his Xbox—was striving toward health.

THROUGHOUT *MASS EFFECT* the player is frequently confronted with choices that influence the way the story proceeds. Consequences can be trivial (a small monetary reward is offered or rescinded), personally significant (a team member loses trust in Shepard or grows closer to him), or heavy with cosmic morality (the last of an imperious alien species is killed or allowed to live). Often these moments of bifurcating paths are clearly demarcated before the player is prompted for input: The player is asked to select, explicitly, whether Shepard drops the remorseful insectoid queen into a vat of acid or lets her go.

Even in less black-and-white situations the game makes an effort to reduce ambiguity. When in dialogue with other characters, the player will sometimes see options glowing blue or red: blue denotes a "paragon" response, signifying noble altruism, while red represents the "renegade" path, signifying firm and occasionally vicious pragmatism. The player is given a choice, but the choice is limited and not nuanced: he has a good sense of the consequences of his actions before being forced to act. Opting for paragon typically leads Shepard toward resolving conflicts through diplomacy, forgiving wrongdoers and holding fast to principles. A renegade Shepard is more likely to resort to threats or violence to deal with conflict and to take an ends-justify-the-means approach to moral problem-solving.

For some players this binary feels imposed and reduction-ist, the product of game design limitations—after all, designers cannot possibly program outcomes for infinite player choices, so the range of interaction must be confined. For a player like Jack, however, the system provided respite from the tumult of his daily life. Jack once expressed profound gratitude for the experience offered to him by *Mass Effect*. "It makes me feel important," he said. "When I see that my paragon score has gone up I know I did a good thing. I know what I'm doing and I know what I'm doing to other people." Coherent social interaction and a sense of competency eluded Jack in daily life but could be found in the sanctuary of game-space.

By inviting Jack's relationship with *Mass Effect* into our thera-peutic relationship, terms like "paragon" and "renegade" naturally became a part of our shared vocabulary.* Either one of us could evoke elements from the game as a bridge to the real world, which seemed a legitimate path to health: if Jack could feel as calm and confident as himself as he did when playing as Shepard, a mul-titude of possibilities might open up for him. The simple act of Jack feeling free to share his virtual self with me brought with it a genuine sense of progress. Jack came to feel that I could see him more clearly in his descriptions of the virtual world—as someone people looked up to, someone in control—than he was used to being seen in the real world, including during the first year of our

---

* All therapies develop a unique common language, at least when the patient–therapist relationship is marked by trust and a sense of purpose. For instance, a patient once described a vivid dream of struggling to scale a brick wall in the middle of a forest and thereafter "climbing the wall" was a phrase to which either one of us might return—useful shorthand for the patient's tendency to put herself in situations that she knew, deep down, would overwhelm her.

therapy. Now, finally, I was bearing witness to the totality of his experience: not only confusion but autonomy, not just frustration but power. More importantly, through my witnessing Jack in this way he became better able to see himself as a complex, three-dimensional human being.

By accepting and expressing curiosity in the part of Jack that was typically relegated to the virtual, he and I developed an increasing ability to compare and contrast his states of being. Over time, Jack found himself less compelled to encroach on my physical space through the use of food and bodily functions and he experienced my interpretations as less violent. We began to discuss the notion of boundaries and how to delineate thought from action and self from other. Jack attributed this shift in relating and understanding in part to us "playing the same game." He had developed an appreciation that I knew his "system" (beginning with *Mass Effect*, then extending to his broader self), which mitigated the need to show me his internal process in his usual intrusive way: he could tell me instead and believed that I would understand.

Externally, many of the dynamics in Jack's life appeared unchanged. Relations with his family remained disturbed and closeness with classmates—including Karen, toward whom he still harbored a deep infatuation—had yet to progress beyond a superficial level. On the inside, however, Jack was starting to see himself as capable of emotional self-regulation and logical decision-making. The fact that he already felt such competency when acting as Shepard proved to be an invaluable link between digital and analogue, a source of evidence that healthful change was possible.

An example of how our appreciation of this link could play itself out: one day we were discussing issues around schoolwork and commuting, but Jack seemed distant, as though uninterested in his own line of thought. After a long pause of staring into the middle distance, he said plainly, "I'm so sick of feeling like this."

"Like what?" I asked.

"I don't know," he replied. "I want a girlfriend, that's all I want. I don't know why it's so hard. When I talk to Karen, everything gets so confusing. She's so hard to read and I don't know what I'm allowed to say. Even if we have a really good talk—like we had this really good conversation last week—five minutes later I start thinking she's changed her mind, so even if she liked me when we were talking now she doesn't like me anymore."

"That must make the idea of pursuing a closer relationship with her pretty overwhelming, if it feels like you're never on solid ground for long."

"It's so confusing. I don't know what I want. No, I think I do know what I want, but I don't know whether I can get it or what it would be like to have it . . . I don't know, I don't know . . ." Jack yawned and stretched in an exaggerated way, as though to declare he was bored, this was boring, let's move on. "I'm so tired," he offered. "I stayed up really late playing *Mass Effect* again."

Because Jack and I both knew that the game had meaning to him inside and outside of our therapy, I didn't take his dismissal of it as an excuse for yawning at face value and said as much: "I don't think it's a coincidence you would bring that up right now. You're talking about how confusing and ambiguous it is when you're with Karen. I bet you wish it were more like it is in *Mass Effect*."

"Well, obviously . . . that would be great! Man, I'm so good at relationships in that game. If I could just see my paragon score when I'm talking to Karen . . ." He laughed and trailed off, his thought incomplete.

"Yeah? Then what?"

Jack considered for a moment. "I wouldn't have to worry so much, I guess. I would know where I stand."

"You feel in control of your relationships in the game," I said. "You feel secure to go around, explore planets, complete missions, without having to worry about people losing interest or changing their minds about you."

"It's crazy. In *Mass Effect* I'm living with all these aliens, but everyone looks up to me. It's so awesome. But in real life I feel alone around other people. Alienated! That's the word, that's exactly how I feel."

For Jack—or anyone contending with a diffusion of internal boundaries—the process of taking a vague, unsettling emotion ("I'm so sick of feeling like this") and giving it a name ("Alienated!") was no small feat. Naming feelings makes them knowable: They become a part of us that can be listened to and understood rather than a frightening invader taking over mind and body. In this instance, Jack and I were able to chart that course between nameless and named through the prism of *Mass Effect*.

Though this was a big deal, it of course didn't solve all of Jack's problems: family and financial issues abounded and cultivating previously arrested interpersonal skills would be a slow, ongoing process. However, the integration of virtual and physical brought a degree of clarity for Jack, a better sense of himself and his emotional life. Not all problems were solved, but he *felt* healthier and so progressively engaged with his life in healthier ways.

Despite often seeing the benefits with my own eyes, I don't prescribe games-playing to anyone in my clinical practice. I take this position for the same reason I don't tell my patients what to do in general: Psychotherapy is a means to feeling more aware and in control of life—*your* life, not mine. My responsibility is to aid people on that journey; I have no right to tell anyone how to live. For Jack, games were essential because he was already living so much of his life inside of them—they represented a direct route to parts of himself that were otherwise difficult to access. Other people benefit from games for precisely the opposite reason: The experience of entering game-space is so novel that it facilitates a kind of contact with the self that had been elusive through more traditional or familiar means. In these cases, my attitude toward games that began with Jack—that is, taking them as seriously as I would any other part of a patient's life—has been essential in allowing patients the space to talk about play, when they might otherwise have been inclined to disregard it as "nothing interesting to say."

SARAH'S LIFE WAS RIDDLED with worry. Each week when she came to see me she felt stricken with some anxiety new or old and, as soon as one concern was quashed, it seemed as though another was lying in wait to fill its place. Her distress typified what I previously referred to as the Winnicottian view of generalized anxiety: Sarah was terrified of that which she could not control. That the world could be unpredictable, or that people might not always abide by the rules, or that some situations might not have well-defined rules to begin with . . . all this was anathema to her. As a result, distant world events or minor issues in Sarah's daily routine alike could catalyze a rapid descent into worry. Every time a terrorist attack was reported on the news Sarah mentally crossed off another line item on the ever-shortening list of places she could go without anxiety—cinemas: out; airplanes: out; tourist attractions: out. Every physical sensation, no matter how benign, coaxed her down the rabbit hole of Google, that winding series of tunnels that invariably led her to the same terminus time and again—headache: cancer; stomachache: cancer; itchy scalp: cancer.

Sometimes Sarah would make light of her experience, sitting down at the start of a session and asking, with a knowing smile, if I was ready to hear her "worry *du jour.*" But when in the throes of anxiety Sarah felt truly debilitated. On one occasion she arrived at my office trembling, barely able to speak through her sobs. She had stopped at a coffee shop near her home on the way, she said, and only upon disembarking her train near my office realized that she had forgotten to pay for her croissant. Immediately, her thoughts had begun to spiral out of control. She worried the baristas would track her down using security footage. She worried she would be arrested and sent to prison. She worried she would never see her wife again. Perhaps above all—because Sarah recognized how disproportionate her anxiety was to the situation, how the facts of her transgression weren't compatible with the severity of the imagined consequences—she worried she was "going crazy."

Ambiguity was Sarah's enemy—or at least she had long convinced herself of that notion. Trying to talk her down from a state of high anxiety by using words like "improbable" or "unlikely" was a fool's errand. Sarah reasoned that if there were a chance of catastrophe, it would be naive—if not downright irresponsible—not to *expect* catastrophe. But living by this creed also exhausted her; she felt deadened, unable to enjoy the present or look forward to the future. Life was little more than the unending exercise of staving off panic.

On another day Sarah began our session with a bemused look on her face and said she had just had a curious experience. At the large advertising firm where she worked, they had installed a virtual reality (VR) booth furnished by a new client that developed VR technology. Even though her work had nothing to do with this client, Sarah and all the other employees were invited to try out this cutting-edge innovation in the gaming medium. Sarah, who had barely touched a videogame in her life, thought it sounded interesting. She put on the headset and launched one of the few demos available, which involved exploring around the ridge of a large canyon. Looking over the precipice of the simulated chasm, she found herself overcome with a visceral fear and awe.

"I would never, ever go to a place like that in real life," she told me. "But it wasn't my usual anxiety, which gnaws at me, drains me of all I've got. Standing at the edge, looking down, I was *scared*. I felt present and alive. It was incredible."

Many people at her office played the same game as her that day, but it is likely that Sarah was the only one to walk away from it feeling as though it had introduced her to a forgotten part of herself. The game did not cure her of her anxiety, but it did provide a new perspective that we were able to use in our treatment. Sarah and I spoke of her canyon adventure in the way we might discuss a dream, as something full of multiple meanings both concrete and symbolic. We could understand the canyon and the giddiness Sarah felt at its edge not only literally as an instinctive reaction to heights—but also as a metaphor for her tendency to avoid certain emotional experiences for fear of losing control of herself—or, as she put it, "falling off a cliff." She had used that very phrase months earlier, in fact, to describe how it had felt to sit quivering in my office, afraid she would be arrested as a pastry thief.

After playing the canyon game, "falling off a cliff" took on new life for us. We recognized that in Sarah's mind there was no differentiation between the fear of falling and the act of falling—in an effort, once again, to reduce ambiguity, she had conditioned herself to conflate the worry of something bad happening with the bad thing itself. The reason why Sarah was so overwhelmed about the croissant wasn't because she thought she was going to be arrested—she knew on a rational level that the idea was outlandish—but because she *felt* as though the arrest had already occurred. Emotionally, Sarah lived catastrophe in advance, as though to preempt the pain of the event that she assumed was perpetually around the corner—to beat it to the punch by punching herself. The virtual canyon, and our discussion of it, helped her to slow down this process. She could appreciate, not only rationally but also emotionally, that there was a difference between standing on the edge and leaping off the side. She had *felt* it, what it was like to be dizzy with fear and then realize that she was still on solid ground. The feeling passed, as feelings were wont to do.

Videogames have an intrinsic dreamlike quality, bounded as they are within the unreality of digital space, where many things are possible, but nothing can leave the confines of the screen. But Sarah and I also had to reconcile the fact that a videogame was not the same as a dream: It was a real thing that existed in the waking world we all share and that required her active participation. Sarah did not conjure up the canyon metaphor purely from within the depths of her unconscious: It was programmed by someone else, and Sarah entered that person's world when she began to play.

She needed the game because she wasn't having the dream: the game brought her into contact with thoughts and feelings that neither the unreality of her inner world nor the reality of her daily life were able to generate on their own. By venturing into the in-between space of the virtual, Sarah reconnected with what was possible when she wasn't siphoning all her energy into anticipating the worst conceivable outcome. Where "falling off a cliff" was certain but fatal, standing on the edge was ambiguous. As Sarah learned to better tolerate that ambiguity she increasingly felt freer to regulate her own anxiety. Rather than leaning further over the edge and accelerating a sense of panic, she could opt to move back a pace or two and grant herself permission to calm down, as nothing catastrophic was happening in the present moment.

In time it became clear to Sarah that her ability to take an ambiguous situation and spin it into all-consuming anxiety was a method of defense. By ensuring, on an unconscious level, that there was always something to worry about, she could avoid the even more frightening emotions that one might find in the act of "leaping": excitement, enthusiasm, joy. The fantasy of being thrown in jail, which cropped up often for Sarah, was inseparable from her fear of being isolated from loved ones, especially her spouse with whom she had a deep and meaningful relationship.

"When I really think about it, the worry isn't about being punished for stealing a croissant," she said some weeks after our discussion of the canyon game. "It's that I'll be punished for being so stupid as to love another person. To care so much about someone even though I can't control—at least not one hundred per cent—if she can be taken away from me."

Sarah inhibited feeling joy, feeling alive, to protect herself from having that feeling stolen from her. It was only after being reminded of what feeling alive was like (via a simulation, para-doxically) that she could start to see how much this once self-pro-tective strategy had run amok. Sarah's instinct to spare herself the pain of loss hadn't spared her at all: Rather, she'd cursed herself to experience that pain over and over again in a kind of practice run for the real thing, even though neither she nor anyone else could say if, when, or how the "real thing" might occur.

Letting go of worry meant letting go of the idea that the fu-ture could be definitively known. Bad things can happen, yes, and such is the ambiguity of life. But so, too, can good things; so, too, can we be struck, like a bolt of lightning, with the spon-taneity of joy.

I HAD PERHAPS NEVER in my life met someone as joyless as Gavin. If Sarah's initial defense against ambiguity had been fear, he instead had opted for surrender: During our first session he told me that he felt like "the universe's punching bag." Even more, at the ripe old age of twenty-nine he said he was resigned to this fate. Nothing, in Gavin's mind, was under his control, but rather than generating anxiety this conviction bred in him a leaden depression. Not only did his job as a graphic designer demand grueling hours while offering menial pay, but it could be ripped from him at a moment's notice through company closure or firing. Even this thing he resented wasn't his, which by exten-sion meant the money he earned there wasn't really his, either, and so neither was the apartment he rented using that money (an apartment that could also be lost in an instant, he figured, through eviction or natural disaster). The idea that he might de-rive meaning or satisfaction from his work, and therefore at least "own" some sense of accomplishment, was laughable to Gavin.

At best he was a cog in a corporate machine: "Cogs are useful, if replaceable," he said. "More likely I'm just a wall decoration and if you removed me it would make no difference at all. The most someone might say is, 'Hey, wasn't there something up on the wall yesterday?' But then they'd probably add, 'It looks better this way.'"

Gavin was vivid, and often bitingly funny, in detailing all the ways his life didn't matter. He epitomized the case of someone who believed he had nothing interesting to say; a thought would scarcely begin to form before Gavin had qualified it to me as "trite" or "full of details so boring you'll think about raising your fee." That he would be forever depressed was unquestionable; the finer point he couldn't quite resolve was whether the source of misery was him or the world. On a day when the woman he'd been dating for years (but refused to move in with on the pretense that doing so would cause her to "wake up" and realize how unbearable he was) surprised him with tickets to see a band they both liked and he struggled to muster a showing of good cheer, Gavin assumed that the defect lay within himself. Other times he might witness a display of rudeness or disrespect between strangers while walking the streets of New York and conclude that, no, it was the world that was irredeemable.

Games entered into our treatment in an unusual way, as they, too, were regarded through Gavin's bleak filter. He told me that in his "younger days" (again, he was twenty-nine) he had found joy and serenity in pursuing various solo activities, chief among them playing videogames. But even that cherished pastime had become sullied over the years and, as with everything else, Gavin went back and forth about which side was to blame. Sometimes he professed a belief that games had warped his social skills by mistakenly teaching him that relationships could be measured reliably and depended upon. The very aspects that Jack had found therapeutic Gavin regarded as a grand deceit: In real life, there was no paragon score. On occasions when Gavin leaned more toward self-blame, the narrative centered around the notion that he simply lacked the capacity to enjoy enjoyable things, like his creative job or thoughtful girlfriend. As a result, he had distanced himself from games over time. He owned no gaming consoles and hadn't regularly played anything in several years.

"Games are supposed to be just for fun," he told me. "If I play them and can't find pleasure in it then it's doubly depressing. It's confirmation that I'm broken."

I have wondered whether it is a distortion of my profession that makes it impossible for me to see something as "just" anything. By insisting there is meaning in play, or in the joy that play generates, am I sucking all the fun out of it? After all, even Freud said that a cigar is sometimes just a cigar;* was Gavin's assertion not reasonable, that sometimes playing a game was "just for fun"? Then again, that still left ambiguous what "just fun" meant or how someone like Gavin might come to see himself as capable of having it (see, I really can't turn it off).

If health is balance, joy is presence: the experience of being in the moment, unburdened by the past and unworried about the future. Health facilitates joy by keeping us away from extremes: It is easier to be present—to keep past and future at bay—if the

---

* This attribution is actually dubious at best. There is no known text in which Freud wrote the line and the first claim that he once said it dates to 1950, more than a decade after Freud's death. So even if a cigar is sometimes just a cigar, a famous quote may not always be what it seems.[68]

stakes feel low. This is precisely how Gavin would come to learn to have fun.

For all his elocutions on the permanence of his misery, Gavin attended our weekly therapy with diligence. He came to sessions on time and without fail and, though he expressed skepticism whenever I challenged one of his more depressive beliefs, he also would often say that he "wanted to believe" me. Some part of him was not wholly committed to an unambiguous future; some part of him believed that change was possible. So, I felt curious, but not altogether shocked, when several months into treatment Gavin announced that he had purchased a Nintendo Switch, his first gaming console since college.

"How do you like it?" I asked.

He looked at me, then looked away. "I'm not sure. I haven't actually turned the thing on yet."

Gavin said he bought the Switch and a game for it, *Super Mario Odyssey,* "on impulse." It didn't seem important to the matter at hand but, in my head, I corrected him. This was not impulse—that is, a leap from feeling to action that bypasses thought—but something more like spontaneity: doing something because he wanted to do it, free of the burden of anticipating dire consequence. Upon receiving the console, however, Gavin's sense of low stakes started to erode and so he had delayed setting it up. He said of the Mario game, "What if I don't like it or I'm bad at it? I'll have wasted the money and tricked myself into thinking I could ever be cheered up."

The gravity Gavin had placed onto the venerable plumber was palpable, like something out of Shakespeare: To play or not to play? That was the question. The answer, it seemed, would directly address an altogether different question, unspoken but implied and much grimmer in tone: Was Gavin incurable?

By chance I had purchased and started *Super Mario Odyssey* at home a week or two earlier and my mind flickered to the virtual world that through Gavin's eyes seemed to carry so much weight. How to even describe the game? Mario teams up with a sentient top hat named Cappy to crash a wedding between a dinosaur and a princess. By tossing Cappy at different objects and creatures in the game's whimsical, technicolor worlds, Mario takes on their characteristics: Throwing the hat on a frog turns Mario into a mustachioed amphibian capable of tremendous vertical leaps; throwing it at a fireball turns Mario into a mustachioed blob of lava capable of traversing rivers of hot magma with ease. In a pure expression of the freewheeling potential of games, the player must transform into whatever is around in order to further explore the current stage and advance to the next one. *Super Mario Odyssey* is hard to take seriously and hard not to smile at; it is an absurd, joyous experience—which made Gavin's severe appraisal of it seem absurd in a different way.

I noted how greatly the prognosis of his health seemed to hinge on a videogame and he was quick to process my comment through his ever-present self-critical filter.

"I know," he said, "it must sound so idiotic, a videogame probably doesn't matter at all . . ."

He was leaping from one extreme to another: first the game was a test to see whether or not he would be depressed forever and now it had zero meaning. I needed to get ahead of Gavin's spiral into shame before he had assimilated the entire act of buying a Nintendo Switch into his old, depressive narrative.

"Look," I said, "let's make one thing perfectly clear. Mario is not a cure for depression."

Gavin laughed. A genuine laugh, full-bodied and spontaneous, the likes of which I had not seen or heard from him before.

I went on. "If you can accept that, it becomes easier to see the game's actual value, which is definitely not everything, but it's not nothing, either."

We had broached this concept before in relation to other topics. But Gavin had deftly countered any claim that behavior related to his relationship or job, say, were low in stakes: these things were important with a capital *I* and how he engaged with them therefore must carry some decree on his worth. If he screwed up at work he was a bad employee, if he upset his girlfriend he was a bad partner. Add enough of these elements together and what other conclusion could one draw but that here was an unambiguously bad human being. Recognizing that he placed that kind of pressure on Mario, however, seemed suddenly unworkable, even to Gavin. As we talked about it, he simply couldn't find a way to rationalize the game as the crucible through which he would be judged. Sometimes Mario was just Mario: Nothing damning could emerge from giving *Odyssey* a go. Worst case, he didn't like it; there were plenty of other games out there to try. Best case, he would have a great time and the game needn't be a palliative for all his woes for that to happen. By the end of our session Gavin said he was looking forward to playing.

"It will probably be fun," he said with a reluctant smile, but a smile nonetheless.

Gavin and I rarely spoke about videogames again for the duration of our treatment. As his ability to enjoy his life and relationships gradually expanded, he would occasionally include games on a list of things that he found satisfying or cite them as useful for coping with stress. Games were never a central part of Gavin's reasons for seeking treatment and they never became a central part of our work. But once he permitted himself to enjoy playing games, they became an important (with a lower-case *i*) part of his definition of a healthy life.

Chapter 8

Multiplayer

What can games teach us about how groups and societies function?

No man is an island entire of itself; every man is a piece of the continent, a part of the main . . .

—John Donne, "No Man Is an Island"

THE CORRIDOR TERMINATED at a door barred with thick iron. Peering through the slats, the brawny monk named Talia saw an eerie green light emitting from the chamber ahead. She and her fellow adventurers heard chittering footsteps along the stone floor, something many-legged and sharp.

"I'm scared," whispered Lord North, the sorcerer. The halfling Darvin drew his short sword and the dwarf priest Kugel said a quick prayer to Dumathoin, his patron deity and god of underground exploration.

The players controlling these characters sat around my living-room coffee table. We were in the midst of our weekly *Dungeons & Dragons (D&D)* game, which I had been running for this group of close friends for years. *D&D* was not a videogame but a tabletop role-playing game: As "dungeon master" (DM) I assumed the responsibilities that in a videogame would default to the computer, namely designing and depicting the world, dictating the actions of non-player characters and arbitrating the rules of play. Rather than using keyboards or controllers to interact, my friends would speak their intentions out loud in conversation. Situations involving probability—such as the likelihood of landing a blow with one's sword, charming someone into doing a favor, or picking a lock—were resolved by dice rolls according to the rules of the *D&D* system.

Talia and company had spent multiple play sessions working their way to this ominous moment. A few weeks back they had stumbled across a murder mystery in the small town of White Haven while on their way to deal with a rumored threat of zombies and necromancy on the continent's southern coast. As professional adventurers, the party was constantly on the lookout for tangential opportunities to test their skills, though each character had his or her own motivation decided freely by the player. Talia and Darvin regarded themselves as moral beings who could not refuse a call to help the endangered or oppressed; Kugel felt no obligation to do good but was willing to endanger his life for the promise of ample monetary reward; Lord North, an outcast from an aristocratic family of elves, thought mostly of restoring his reputation.

Despite these differences, the group had worked well together over the past couple of months since we had started this new campaign,* deftly navigating the obstacles I had thus far placed in their path. A large part of the camaraderie and agreement among the characters, of course, was attributable to the fact that the

---

* Usually once every year or so my weekly *D&D* group and I would conclude that our current game had run its course. Players might have grown bored of their characters or I might have felt that I had exhausted stories to tell within this iteration of the fantasy world. Sometimes we would take a break and play or do other things for a while, but inevitably we'd return to *D&D*, they with fresh characters and me with a fresh world and storyline for them to explore.

players were all friends in real life; no matter how diametrically opposed the values of their characters might have been, we all had a long history of getting along. This compatibility was something that I treasured in our friendships but had grown tiresome to me as a DM and, in this current adventure, I quietly hoped to test the boundaries of kinship within the boundaries of the game.

The murder investigation had led the party to suspect that a sinister force was at work in White Haven, pulling strings with law enforcement and keeping the populace terrified. They discovered a secret entrance to an underground labyrinth beneath the town, at the bottom of which they suspected this mastermind was hiding. It took my friends two sessions—a real-time total of about six or seven hours—to work through the labyrinth, rife with traps and patrolled by a guilt-ridden minotaur. Now they had descended further to the workshop of the villain they sought. Talia opened the creaky gate.

In a domed chamber filled with equipment suggesting dark alchemical practices stood the target of the group's weeks-long search: a tall, graceful creature wearing a flowing black robe, with purplish skin and small tentacles writhing around the bottom of his face like a living beard. About his feet a pulsing brain with spidery legs ending in talons scampered like a pet chihuahua. The figure in robes was a mind flayer, a classic monster from the *D&D* pantheon, typically an intelligent and vainglorious enemy who has the grotesque ability to scoop out and devour a character's brain whole.

He—that is, I—greeted the adventurers warmly. He'd anticipated their arrival, he said, and knew that before being waylaid in White Haven they had been en route further south. He, too, was concerned about the necromantic rumors coming from the far end of the continent and would like to help the characters reach their goal and deal with this problem. With their consent, he would be happy to open up a portal that would zap them directly to the southern coast, saving them weeks or months of in-game travel. As for whatever he was up to in this deep sub-basement filled with unnatural green light . . . the adventurers needn't worry about it, it was none of their concern.

Here was the scenario that I had been waiting to use to ensnare my friends. They had an ambiguous decision to make and, as anticipated, that meant they did not instantly share an idea of what to do next.

"What should we do?" Talia asked the rest.

"I don't think we're supposed to fight him, he looks too powerful." This was not Lord North speaking but David, the man who played as Lord North. David was engaging in a process known in role-playing patois as meta-gaming: Rather than speaking and acting on behalf of his character within the game world, he was trying to figure out the system, *my* system; he wanted in this moment to master the scenario rather than play freely within it. It was precisely to combat this sort of behavior that I had designed the encounter with the mind flayer to be vague, a gambit that quickly proved successful, when Molly, who played as Kugel, cut in.

"What do you mean we're not supposed to fight him? We just spent all this time getting down here so we *could* fight him." She turned to me, speaking now for Kugel. "I ready my hammer."

"Whoa, whoa, whoa!" cried Joanna and Eric in unison, playing as Talia and Darvin respectively. Talia continued, "Let's not be hasty. We don't know for certain that this thing is guilty of anything worth dying for."

"Also, guys," Darvin said, "I don't know if I wanna walk all the way to the south coast."

"Why should we trust him?" David said, reentering as the acerbic Lord North. "He's clearly a creepy weirdo with an animate brain for a pet. Then again, if we defeat him the townspeople will probably celebrate us as heroes . . ."

"I suggest you take me up on my generous offer," I said, as the mind flayer. "Alternately, you are free to go back out the way you came. Any aggressive action you might be considering would be . . . ill-advised."

From my point of view, as the omniscient DM, I knew that the characters would be permitted to leave peacefully, though this would be a profoundly demoralizing end to their efforts. They were also free to fight the mind flayer, but it would be a difficult battle; most likely one or more of them would be literally brainless before it was over. These options and the risks or disappointments involved seemed fairly clear to my friends, as well. The path I was most interested in seeing them negotiate was going through the mind flayer's portal. If they took a moment to calmly consider, it was by far the worst option. They would be putting themselves entirely at the mercy of a shifty creature they did not know and, in fact, had every reason to believe was holding the town above in the grip of terror.

But the conversation was heating up, so a moment of reasonable consideration never arrived. Lord North and Kugel didn't want to die; Talia and Darvin refused to retreat. Feeling implicit pressure from me to make a choice and unusually out of sync with each other, Joanna turned to me and, speaking for Talia and the rest while trying in vain to read my facial expressions, declared that the group would go through the portal.

It was, of course, a trick. After joining hands and being swept into a break in time and space created by the mind flayer, the characters emerged to find themselves trapped in a hell dimension filled with menacing devils. It would take them many real-world weeks to find their way back out.

At the end of the play session Eric, no longer channeling Darvin, was genuinely irate. "What the hell, guys!" he shouted in an incidental pun on their new predicament. "Why did we go through that portal? That was such an obviously stupid thing to do. Who was pushing for that?"

Everyone agreed their decision had been illogical, yet no one could quite recall by what means they had arrived at it. Privately, I felt a twinge of guilt over my calculated plot to mess with their cooperative dynamic. We all bounced back quickly enough, the bonds of friendship outside the game being far stronger than the now-frayed ones within it but, for the rest of the evening, at least, a pall lingered. How easy it had been for the gossamer separating self from group to dissolve, and easier still for that group to careen toward destruction.

In time this would become a celebrated moment in our shared gaming history—we all came to appreciate the opportunity to grapple with emotional decision-making that felt real for a moment and then could be left peacefully within game-space. But though the safety of play meant no lasting wounds were inflicted, the group dynamics in that *D&D* session evoked questions about how people live and play with each other. This book's exploration up to this point, given its focus on solitary, single-player gaming, has not broached this area. How did my friends come to collectively make a choice that individually they all thought was a mistake? Why did I feel guilty about tricking them despite there being no real-world consequences?

✳

Groups are hard. In *Civilization and its Discontents*, Freud wrote about the inherent tension in society between order and chaos, portraying modernity as a constant struggle to strike a balance between the craving of the id and the micromanaging of the superego.[69] While those classical terms have fallen out of fashion in recent decades,* Freud's observation that groups large and small have a tendency to exert bizarre influence on individual members resonates as profoundly today—if not more so—as it did when his book was first published in 1930. He had watched from his Viennese window as Europe nearly burned itself to the ground during World War I, a mind-bending chapter in history in which unprecedented levels of group coordination were leveraged toward unprecedented levels of group destruction. On a scale exponentially larger and more consequential, Freud asked a similar question as that which emerged from the *D&D* game my friends and I had played together: How were so many individuals corralled into behavior that imperiled the very existence of those individuals? Freud's proposed answer in his book was what he called a "death drive," an innate and unconscious psychological urge to return to the nothingness whence we came. This drive attempted to explain not only more obviously self-destructive behaviors like charging into a war zone, but the very pull to-

---

* For good reason, in many cases. Freud spent much of his career in search of universal truths, ways to describe psychological experience that he believed were immutable and held fast across all individuals. While some fundamental psychoanalytic concepts (like the unconscious) have stood the test of Freud's ambition over time, others have not. The triptych of id (the part of the mind that pushes the self to seek pleasure), superego (the part of the mind that pushes the self to obey social rules) and ego (the part of the mind that tries to satisfy the demands of both id and superego while interacting with reality) is now undoubtedly better thought of as a metaphor—one possible lens through which to view the mind, rather than a factual depiction of how all minds are structured.

ward group membership in general. We all, on some level, wish to surrender our individual selves to what Freud referred to as the "oceanic" feeling of belonging to something greater.[70]

The death drive provoked much debate and head-scratching in the psychoanalytic community at the time and in retrospect it seems clear that Freud's concept was at least as much a glimpse into his desperation to explain the unexplainable horrors of war as it was a reasoned hypothesis. Yet Freud was not the only theorist to observe the paradox of the group, an entity that so often brings people together in order to tear other people apart. Evolutionary biologists and poets alike have on one hand pointed out the frightening power of the collective, while on the other hand pondered whether a human being in isolation is truly human at all.

Existential philosophers like Jean-Paul Sartre[71] and psychotherapists like Rollo May[72] have suggested an alternative to an inborn death drive as a means to explain the group paradox. Namely, that the responsibility of free will generates a paralyzing anxiety that demands resolution: To accept that we can do what we want with our lives is to accept that we are accountable if things don't work out. For some, the solution to this angst is to give up control of their lives to the will of a group, outsourcing individual freedom and responsibility in one fell swoop, whether to a religious or political organization, a domineering family structure, or otherwise.

Existentialism, particularly as a theory of psychotherapy, emerged in large part as a kind of riposte to the institution of psychoanalysis in the mid-twentieth century. Where Freud focused on "psychic determinism"—the idea that much of who we are and what we do is dictated not by conscious will but unconscious motivation—the existential perspective highlighted the human capacity for self-direction and meaning-making. It is all the more notable, then, that both schools of thought arrived at similar conclusions surrounding groups: that they are needed for survival and a sense of purpose yet are also dangerous for their tendency to make us forget ourselves, our autonomy and the autonomy of others.

No matter where we fall on the spectrum of existential freedom to paralysis, we all define ourselves to some degree by group membership: by family name, nationality, religion, political affiliation and countless other identities adopted as a means of feeling like we belong with certain people (and, often, like we don't belong with others). Groups breed affinity and warmth, but also competition and violence. Many groups coexist and intermingle, others turn on each other, and still others turn on themselves.

Freud saw the individual's natural desire for freedom and uniqueness as being in direct conflict with the group's desire for control and sameness. As a result, human civilization exists in a state of perpetual tension, at the center of which is the experience of guilt. Unlike the previously discussed feeling of shame, which is the internalization of being made to feel that one is bad at the core, guilt is the internalization of the group—or more specifically of responsibility *to* the group, often according to the standards set by our parents and society at large. When the pursuit of individual gratification compels us toward an action that would harm others, guilt has the power to give us pause.

Individuals who never internalize the group are, from this perspective, dangerous free radicals. At the most extreme they can be serial murderers, rapists, or abusers who pursue their instincts with no regard for the basic rights of others. In the language of games, we would call these people "cheaters." Cheating goes beyond breaking the rules of a game (though it usually involves this); it is the process of violating the space that makes play possible. When someone kills another person in the real world, our horror and outrage is not over the fact that a law against murder was disregarded; most of us do not need such laws as a deterrent. The act itself represents an affront to the mutually agreed-upon space that we call society, a space in which, ideally, we are freely permitted to live and explore what it means to be alive. Unfortunately, people cheat all the time—in different ways and to greater or lesser degrees—making equality and safety perpetually out of civilization's reach and requiring vigilant group oversight in the form of laws and people deputized to enforce those laws (both of which, of course, have the potential to overstep their bounds and unfairly restrict certain people's freedom).

Individuals on the other end, who excessively internalize the strictures of the group, are the inverse of cheaters: They take play (and life) so seriously and regard the stakes of their actions as being so high that they are beset by depression, anxiety, and self-reproach. They police themselves, administering punishment for private thoughts and feelings as though they have committed crimes in the real world. They cannot play, or be playful, for fear of incurring the wrath of a critical, disappointed authority.

From Freud's point of view, the group—from its smallest manifestation in a *D&D* game to the most abstract notion of society—is a necessary evil: a watchful, often oppressive force that keeps the individual in check by stoking guilt in moments when he might be tempted to follow instinctual urges that bear antisocial consequences. Civilization is walking a razor's edge between the anarchy of unbridled gratification and the fascism of groupthink—to use Freud's analogy, like living in a conquered town occupied by a garrison of soldiers.* Society, like the individual, struggles with balancing needs and desires both conscious and unconscious—unfortunately, unlike individuals, there is no known therapy to treat a society. It was on this note that Freud left us in his book, quickly proffering in its final pages an unconvincing optimism that "one day somebody"[73] would make inroads toward better understanding not only what holds the fabric of civilization together, but what could help civilization move toward healthier ways of being.

We may safely assume Freud would be surprised to learn that one of the best current avenues for such understanding is not the work of a great scientist or philosopher, but a massive online videogame set twenty thousand years in the future.

As MY COMFORT WITH TALKING and writing about the intersection of psychology and videogames increased over the years, colleagues started deferring to me as a gaming expert in clinical matters. There was, however, a major element of games with which I was still relatively unfamiliar: the social element. Games had always been a private pursuit for me; I had never invested time in popular titles like *Fortnite* or *World of Warcraft (WoW)*, in which hundreds, thousands, or even millions of players cooperate and compete within the same digital world. I might have

---

* Ironically, Freud, a secular Jew, was so convinced of the totalitarian potential of organized religion—the Catholic church in particular—that he all but dismissed the rise of Nazi fascism in Germany and his home country of Austria. He was only barely convinced to flee to England in 1938 before dying of cancer in 1939. Freud would therefore never know how terribly accurate his fears of the group had been—even as compared to the destruction he'd witnessed firsthand during the preceding world war—though those fears had been levied at that time toward the wrong group.

dominion over an entire society in a game such as one from the *Sid Meier's Civilization* series, but my allies and opponents alike were computer-controlled, algorithmic in all the ways that the unpredictable whims of other people were not.

I typically preferred an isolationist approach anyway: In 2010's *Civilization 5* my de facto avatar was Gandhi, leader of the Indian people, who came with a special ability that made it easier to grow a small number of cities into bustling metropolises without needing to expand physical territory. This meant I could find a small patch of resource-rich land, hopefully surrounded by water or impassable mountains, and build up a productive society while avoiding warring or trading with neighboring civilizations as much as possible. If Montezuma or Catherine the Great came knocking with proposals for diplomatic exchange, my awareness that I was negotiating with a computer—not real people—always made it a little easier to send them packing, disappointed and vaguely threatening some future military aggression.

Even tabletop games like *D&D* I largely avoided until adulthood, so long held was my internalized shame over being interested in play. Once my friends and I began those weekly sessions when I was in my mid-twenties, our real-world closeness always felt like an essential ingredient to me. I could reduce anxieties around being judged, criticized, or rejected and let flow my creative ideas—such as the devious plot of teleporting my friends to hell—if I knew that the relationships within the game were buoyed by stable, long-standing ones outside of the game. Many people share this attitude with regard to videogames and choose to engage in multiplayer scenarios—whether the focused skirmishes of a first-person shooter like *Call of Duty* or the more open-ended adventuring of a massively multiplayer online game (MMOG) like *WoW*—only with people they know in real life, even if during play each person sits in his or her respective home, connected to one another through a shared online server. But countless others are happy to connect with strangers in virtual space. By pitting up to a hundred players against one another, the extremely popular *Fortnite* practically ensures that you will have to encounter players you don't know, and lasting bonds often form based entirely on the common activity of playing the game.

Jack and I shared an aversion to the multiplayer experience. After games in general and *Mass Effect* in particular had long been a part of our work, Jack introduced a new title into our shared space called *EVE Online*. Unlike previously discussed games, however, Jack had barely played *EVE* and emphatically did not like it—it was, however, a significant passion for Karen, the woman for whom Jack held romantic feelings and with whom he was perpetually seeking a way to spend more time.

On the surface it may have appeared odd that Jack had little interest in *EVE*, especially given his love for *Mass Effect*. Both were set in the distant future and revolved around traveling across a fictional galaxy and slowly growing one's character through exploration, diplomacy and combat; both existed in large virtual worlds that invited players to spend many hours within them. Nevertheless, Jack had two primary objections. The first was a matter of system: The way the player engaged with each game could scarcely have been further apart. *Mass Effect*'s system was designed to make the player feel like the star of a science-fiction story: fast combat, tense confrontations, a new mission waiting in every port. *EVE* was designed less for playability than realism: Its system was intended to simulate what it would be like to try to make a name and living for oneself in an outer-space society filled with other people trying to do the same thing. The difference between *Mass Effect* and *EVE* was the difference between a day in the life of Indiana Jones versus that of an actual archaeologist.

Jack's second issue with *EVE* resonated personally with me: you could only play it with other people. Many games with multiplayer components, including MMOGs, allow the player to participate on his own to greater or lesser degrees. Shooters like those in the *Call of Duty* series feature single-player story campaigns that exist completely separately from the competitive dogfights of their multiplayer modes. In *WoW* the only way to play the game is to go online, and there are certain areas so difficult that they essentially require working with others, and other areas where the player can be directly attacked by other human players. But *WoW* also features a plethora of storylines and adventures that a player may pursue solo, in which he chiefly engages with computer-controlled environments and characters as he would in any single-player title. Often the early phases of MMOGs are set up this way, so that the player has time to learn the ropes, improve his character and start getting to know other players before being thrown into the full social world of the game.

Not so with *EVE*. The computer provides little purpose to the player: while pre-written missions and computer-controlled characters exist, they are chiefly regarded as methods to earn income so that a player can more competently engage with the game's vast social universe. To play *EVE* is to emigrate to a new world composed of thousands of star systems and hundreds of thousands of players, replete with complex economies and dense networks of player-run groups and subgroups—referred to as "corporations"—working together and against one another to survive and thrive. Jack found it, in a word, overwhelming.

He first brought the game up in session, however, in the context of an intriguing invitation from Karen. She knew how much he loved games and also his relative lack of familiarity with *EVE:* maybe they could play together sometime and she could show him how it works? Jack was visibly thrilled to be relaying this development to me; it was precisely the move toward greater intimacy that he felt ready for, an opportunity to share and be together that was still distinct from any overt romantic or sexual overture, the idea of which still caused Jack a great deal of anxiety. At the same time, he was already trying to devise ways that he and Karen could bond over *EVE* without his having to play it very much. He knew, and said plainly, that simulation-heavy titles were not for him. Games, as he and I had discussed at length, were a way for Jack to reduce complexity and in so doing regulate his mood and anxiety levels. A game like *EVE*—with its internal stock markets and political campaigns—defeated the purpose for him. I left our session curious about *EVE* and shortly thereafter decided, in my private time, to conduct a deep dive into its world. It was one I knew so little about—indeed, a single world within a galaxy of multiplayer worlds, most of which felt alien to me. What I found was one of the most fascinating examples of a videogame's capacity to simulate the richness and ugliness of human society, which in turn had the potential to teach us something about why we make the collective choices we make on scales large and small. *EVE* varies from other MMOGs on an important technical level. Most titles, such as *WoW,* spread players out across many different servers. While there may be hundreds of thousands or even millions of active players, the game is essentially splintered into several identical instances, with players distributed throughout; the world any given player inhabits is therefore likely shared by hundreds or thousands—not hundreds of thousands—of other players. Functionally, this places a firm limit on the impact players can have on the world of the game. A player may form small adventuring parties or join larger guilds, she may forge alliances or start conflicts with others, but these interactions are bound to the server on which that player is hosted—the scores of players hosted elsewhere have no way of seeing the player or the consequences of her in-game behavior, indeed have no way of knowing she even exists. The only way all *WoW* players can experience the same event in unison is if it is dispersed to all servers by the game's developer, Blizzard Entertainment, the unequivocal holder of the keys to the kingdom.

EVE, by contrast, exists on a single server; any event that occurs between players therefore takes place in the same version of the world as experienced by all other players.* As a result, since its launch in 2003 *EVE* has developed a reputation as a vast social experiment in which the will and actions of players hold tremendous sway, sometimes far more than those of the developer, CCP Games. CCP has also famously adopted a hands-off approach to player behavior, encouraging people to test the boundaries of what is both possible and ethical within the game. For years *EVE*-related news stories have often looked like they belonged on the front page of a national newspaper, if not for their taking place in a virtual world: a crooked entrepreneur shorts the commodity

---

* There is one notable exception: Players based in China are hosted on a separate server due to their country's strict internet regulations.

market by buying cheap stock before blowing up his own mining operation; a manhunt comes to fruition after two years thanks to a vigilant watchdog group with members in nearly every time zone; activists reveal that a former high-level politician was involved in proliferating illegal riot-control gear; a battle claims thousands of lives and costs billions.*

EVE functions like a laboratory for real-world social issues. Though the notion of outer-space factions vying for economic supremacy could be easily dismissed as frivolous, it should be regarded as anything but. The game provides unprecedented data on how thousands of people come together to deal with everything from crime to diplomacy—nebulous concepts that are notoriously difficult for social scientists to research, requiring either crude approximation within university lab settings or waiting for large-scale events to occur in the real world and then hoping to gain access to relevant data. In *EVE,* major occurrences like wars, trade agreements, and the unravelling of diplomatic alliances are freely traceable through streams of the game and analyses taking place in various corners of the internet. The decision-making and group dynamics between virtual heads of state and their constituents do not take place behind closed doors: players often post online before, during, and after significant in-game events to elucidate their thought processes. The conscious distinction between real and virtual, player and character, engenders a sense

---

* Everything in *EVE* has an appraised value in ISK, the in-game currency. Wars, thefts, trades and so on can therefore all be attributed concrete monetary worth, much in the same way we evaluate these events in the real world. Even more, *EVE* has long allowed its players to pay for their monthly game subscription fees using ISK, effectively giving the game's currency an exchange rate to real money (though ISK cannot be spent outside the game in any other way). As a result, headlines such as "virtual war costs $300,000 in damages" tend to crop up when news outlets cover what's going on in *EVE*.

of lowered stakes that in turn allows greater transparency than real-world global events often afford.

A key leader in a devastating conflict between warring factions may freely confess in a blog post that a battle that left thousands of his fellow characters dead was not motivated by a desire to secure valuable resources in an enemy-occupied sector, as advertised through official channels—rather, he was acting on a personal vendetta against an enemy leader, who months earlier shorted him on a spaceship trade. An honest disclosure such as this sets off a chain reaction, as others from the *EVE* community contribute their reflections from their perspective as players invested in the game world but also existing outside it. Some are incensed for pragmatic reasons: They lost valuable assets and time as a result of being misled. Others are nonplussed: They rely on the corporation for economic security and in return fight on its behalf; the reason why is immaterial. Still others express a sense of disillusionment: They play *EVE* in search of that "oceanic" feeling; they had wanted to believe that they were part of something bigger, something unified. Taken together, this blending of in-game action and out-of-game reflection grants unique insight into the decisions we make as part of a group: how a single individual can derail a multitude; how, when faced with the pressure of joining or defying the group, individual psychologies coalesce along lines of practicality, loyalty, and faith to rationalize decisions.

In 2013 the United Nations granted *EVE* a World Summit Award, which the organization described as recognition for digital work demonstrating a "high impact on improving society."[74] One YouTube commentator framed the accolade in the UN-friendly language of education and diplomacy, saying that "although *EVE Online* takes place in a virtual universe, it allows people to understand not only more of how the world economy works, but specifically why parts of the economy are regulated."[75] A player writing on an *EVE* message board proffered an alternate explanation of the game's impact in improving society: "It [lets] us hunt, extort, scam, torture, humiliate, and publicly demean each other. If there wasn't *EVE,* we'd probably be doing the same to random people we meet."[76]

What makes the social and political web of *EVE* instructive (and enjoyable) to read about and watch is the fact that its players are voluntary participants in its unique brand of large-scale world-building: It is a collectively agreed experiment in civility and disorder. The player above alluded to the psychoanalytic notion of displacement: *EVE* offered him a safe place to explore socially taboo activities alongside people who have also opted in to explore those and other experiences. This is useful not only in and of itself as a source for catharsis (for players) and group behavior data (for social scientists and other interested observers), but also because *EVE* and games like it provide concrete opportunities to draw a clear boundary between play and abuse.

In a detailed account for *PC Gamer* in 2017, journalist Steven Messner laid out a remarkable series of events in *EVE* involving elements ubiquitous to the game—duplicity, tyranny, and chivalry but also very real abuse. At the heart of the story was a player with the handle Scottmw15, who recruited new players to join his corporation, transported them to Russian-occupied space (as in, all players in the area were Russian-speaking in the real world other than those within Scottmw15's corporation, which was English-speaking) and then forced them to engage in menial labor in order to enhance his character's personal wealth. Refusal meant that players' characters would be cut loose into space with no money or resources to leave a sector filled with hostile forces who literally did not speak the same language. Players hung on to vague promises that they would one day be promoted to more interesting and lucrative positions within the corporation. As Messner put it, "Scottmw15 wasn't running a corporation, he was running a forced labor camp."[77]

This situation would strike many who don't play *EVE* as ludicrous, but in abstract it holds a definitive place within the game's ethos. Even new players anticipate that they will have to scrape their way to a position of means and in doing so may find themselves trapped, tricked, or otherwise degraded. Players stayed with Scottmw15, at least initially, because this was part of what they signed up for: a simulation of working one's way up from nothing.

Over time, however, Scottmw15 broke the unspoken laws that permitted players to experience a virtual recreation of oppression and bondage without becoming overwhelmed by it. In the midst of being harangued by outside factions—threatening his in-game livelihood—Scottmw15 began lashing out at his "employees," trampling the boundary between player and character in the process. In one notable example Scottmw15 publicly taunted another player for his cancer diagnosis, something that the player had told Scottmw15 about in confidence during an online chat outside the game. The shared fantasy spoiled, several players left *EVE* entirely out of exhaustion and disgust.

Eventually, an elaborate rescue effort was engineered by a veteran player named Scooter McCabe who had caught wind of how Scottmw15 was treating other players; Scottmw15 fled the game as those he'd enslaved were liberated and invited into other corporations. Scooter tied his motivation to intervene to a recognition that Scottmw15's behavior crossed a line from simulation to something all too real, something abusive, behavior that was "actively hurting the game itself."[78] Scottmw15 had not cheated, per se: no technical rules of the game had been exploited in his operation. But he had violated the spirit of the game and the boundaries that allowed play and social relationships to safely flourish.

Abuse is not part of play but rather is antithetical to it, destroys it, and this is perhaps the most important message to be communicated to our children, students, partners, and friends who participate in online gaming. *Play is consensual, abuse is not.* Play may often involve behaviors that look abusive to an outside observer—such as simulated violence—but if all parties agree to participate and there is an understanding of the line between play and reality, the experience can ultimately be enjoyable and prosocial, even illuminating. If play involves the creation of potential space to facilitate safe exploration of self and other, then abuse occurs when potential space breaks down: an abuser violates the game's potential *by attacking the player instead of the player's character.* In turn the victim is robbed of the sense of safety that game-space ideally provides—the safety to be who they want to be.

When an individual is targeted for who they are, a game is no longer being played: The veil has been torn and all players are now simply people connected online or otherwise in the real world, and in the real world there is the potential for real harm. Abuse is sometimes defended as an inherent part of gaming culture, as if to suggest that holding players to a basic standard of decency is unreasonable. This is pure rationalization, an attempt to skip over thinking about antisocial behavior in the interest of justifying it. Phrases like "boys will be boys" have been employed for the same purpose from time immemorial.

When abuse is identified in games and in life, intervention is required—both sides need to be reminded of the boundaries of play and healthy social interaction. The victim of abuse needs to know that how she was treated is not normal and that feeling overwhelmed does not indicate weakness or hypersensitivity; it is a natural reaction to having one's sense of safety and personal integrity violated. The perpetrator of abuse needs to know, in a sense, that civilization is watching: Behavior that actively harms others will not be ignored and the individual will be held accountable for his actions.

In the short term, ensuring that victims are distanced—physically or virtually—from an abuser is the priority. Once immediate safety is established, those involved with the abuser (or responsible for him, if he is a child), such as therapists, parents, or friends, can more readily take an empathic stance. Why did this person choose to shatter the play space? What were they trying to accomplish or communicate and how can those needs be addressed without jeopardizing the liberty and well-being of others?

JACK BARELY MENTIONED *EVE* AGAIN—in a graceful maneuver indicative of his progress, he suggested to Karen that she teach him how to play *League of Legends* instead, a different online game that she also knew much more about than did Jack, but which he found more appealing than *EVE*. Sparks didn't instantly fly, but the two of them established a regular get-together that Jack found exciting and grounding; it became easier for him to conceptualize being in a stable relationship with Karen, rather than a fickle and unknowable other.

My next encounter with *EVE* came serendipitously a few months later in the same clinic where I worked with Jack, in the context of a psychotherapy group I co-led for individuals dealing with serious medical conditions. It turned out to be a prime example not only of the border between play and abuse, but of the potential for therapeutic intervention to heal and educate once that border is crossed.

Nell was a woman in her mid-thirties, in the early stages of organ rejection following a kidney transplant less than a year earlier. Before I knew her, she had been on dialysis for two years and had been making her way, at long last, to the top of the transplant list that held the promise of reversing a prematurely infirm existence. Instead, the transplant had brought its own host of complications and a sharp decrease in optimism that life would one day be easier. When I met her, Nell rarely left the house except for essential errands, medical appointments, and to attend our weekly group; she presented with feelings of depression and hopelessness, chronic pain, and a deep sense of shame about her body. She had put on a great deal of weight in recent months, in part due to fluid retention from her kidney issues but also due to the fact that she had let slip her healthy routines in diet and exercise as it became clear that her transplant had not been an unambiguous success.

Other members of the group each contended with their own medical struggles and all were between the ages of twenty-five and forty-five. A common theme in our discussions was that of young lives robbed of their potential. Two women were diagnosed with multiple sclerosis; another woman had the autoimmune disease lupus; one man was dying of a late-stage lymphoma; another was awaiting a heart transplant and came to sessions wearing a heavy vest housing a machine that pumped his blood for him.

My approach to group work has been profoundly influenced by the writing of Wilfred Bion,[79] one of the major theorists in psychoanalysis (or elsewhere) to take up Freud's call for "one day somebody" to consider groups seriously as an object of psychological study. Bion once wrote that a group "is more than the aggregate of individuals, because an individual in a group is more than an individual in isolation."[80] He was not only channeling the poet John Donne's notion that "no man is an island"; Bion specifically meant to suggest that an individual in a group is not a single, ossified thing, but a range of possibilities. Unlike Freud, who wrote abstractly of society and civilization, Bion had witnessed through his experience running psychotherapy groups how the same physical assemblage of people could at different times and under different conditions become entirely different "group animals."[81]

Ideally, a therapist would endeavor to facilitate what Bion called "work groups," in which the collective functions as a cohesive whole in the service of helping each individual member address his or her issues.* Work groups take time and trust to achieve and maintain—even though one would think that therapists and patients alike would want to work together in a collaborative and supportive fashion all the time. Bion saw group dynamics as something more like a tightrope walker constantly under threat of falling to one side (self-preservation at the ex-

---

* Given how we have defined play as a collaborative, healthful experience that takes place in a safe, mutual space, we might aptly rename Bion's ideal "play groups."

pense of the group) or the other (group preservation at the expense of the self), either of which had the potential to dissolve the group entirely. Bion noted that, paradoxical though it may seem, group members would routinely abandon the reason they were in the group (to try to improve their outside lives) in order to draw attention (consciously or unconsciously) to situations perceived to endanger the survival of the group itself.

Work groups could quickly transform into something more chaotic, inhibited, or adversarial in the face of disturbances created by a rule-breaker (such as a member who missed sessions, showed up late, dominated conversations, or rarely spoke at all), a splintered faction (such as two members who flirted or picked fights with one another, excluding other members), or a loss of safety (such as a violent outburst in group, the death of a group member, or a lack of faith that the therapist would be able to handle these or similar potentialities).

The group I led that included Nell fit snugly into Bion's perspective; the mutual collaboration of a work group, in which the energy of all was leveraged to ease suffering—individually and collectively—felt like a summit we occasionally reached but where we rarely lingered. Given the medical issues that defined group membership, events like a member not showing up one week were fraught and difficult to discuss: anger and hurt that one person had not upheld their commitment to attend was complicated by anxieties that the person was not present due to a flare-up in illness or worse. At its best, however, the group took on the form of a genuine community; members felt a kinship toward each other that was difficult to find with others, even family and friends, whose bodies had not seemingly gone into revolt.

Over the course of my first few months running the group, members openly expressed concern about Nell, who seemed more depressed, lethargic, and resigned with each passing week. They experimented with offering sympathy for her predicament, admonishments for her "giving up" and practical tips to get her out of the house more often. Nothing seemed to gel and Nell's discouragement became the group's discouragement. Our inability to help Nell cast a pall on the work as a whole—an uneasy, unspoken doubt about whether this group could help anyone began to form. One day when Nell showed up thirty minutes into the sixty-minute session, Lucy (the woman with lupus) could not conceal her rage.

"You better have a good fucking explanation for waltzing in here halfway through," she said, before Nell had even sat down. "I don't know what makes you think this is OK. We've all been here—where the hell were you?"

This was Lucy's way of abandoning the work group to draw everyone's attention to a perceived threat. If Nell could be positively identified as the dysfunctional piece of the whole, perhaps the whole could be spared by attacking and ostracizing the piece. The other members were, understandably, immediately set on edge. Cohesion and safety had been replaced by one member implicitly demanding they take sides, by sharing in Lucy's anger, quietly condoning it by saying nothing or coming to Nell's defense.

"I'm sorry," Nell replied, not sounding particularly sorry. "I got caught up in *EVE*."

Nell had never mentioned *EVE* or any videogame in group before and I suspected that this terse reply was intended to be confusing—to unbalance Lucy with an excuse she wouldn't understand and so could not condemn out of hand.

"Did you say *EVE?*" I asked. "I didn't know you played *EVE Online,* Nell."

I wish I could say this was a fully thought-out intervention, but in truth I think I spoke to buy time as much as anything else. I was hesitant to confront Lucy's outburst while she was still visibly flushed with anger; I also wanted to address Nell's lateness without falling into the trap of taking sides.

Nell appeared mortified, as if I had outed her—she obviously had not anticipated that I would be familiar with the game. She folded her arms across her chest and said, "I don't want to talk about it."

"You brought it up," I replied. "And you know how disruptive it is to arrive in the middle of a session. You don't have to explain yourself—"

"Yes, she does," Lucy cut in.

"No," I said. "No one here is obligated to say anything they don't want to say. Nell doesn't have to explain being late, but"—I turned to her—"you do need to take responsibility for it."

If guilt is the glue holding civilization together, here I was actively trying to guilt Nell. She was clearly feeling disconnected from the group and the group was struggling to identify how to feel about her. I hoped that if Nell could access her internalization of the group she would be reminded of how worried everyone must have been about her absence, which in turn might lead her to reengage with the group in a more relatable way.

"I am sorry," Nell said in a more genuine tone. "I realize I probably just interrupted a whole discussion and I don't want to take all the attention, that doesn't seem fair."

Ricardo, the man with lymphoma, leaned in. "Now, wait, I want to understand what you guys are talking about. What did you say you were doing before you came in, Nell?"

Nell sighed. "I was just playing this game I like, it's called *EVE Online*. I don't usually play it the mornings we have group but some friends had all planned to log in so we could do something together, in the game."

Ricardo leaned back, appearing satisfied. "See, I haven't seen you smile like that in months," he said. It was true: Simultaneously we all seemed to process, Nell included, that Nell was smiling.

"And since when do you have friends?" another group member called Catherine added, and then laughed. "Oh, god, I didn't mean it like that. But I've literally never heard you talk about friends before."

Nell proceeded, with increasing animation, to describe her relationship with *EVE*. In stark contrast to how we had known her in group, inside the game she lived an inverted existence of popularity and confidence, the leader of a small band of space pirates. She had built a character to her specifications and engaged with people over shared objectives—unlike most of Nell's other social interactions, which happened within the hospital and were confined to investigating the state of her physical and mental health. We bore witness each week to "sick" Nell and, indeed, she had seemed to grow progressively sicker, in body and spirit, every time we saw her. But sequestered entirely from our group space was a "not-sick" Nell who thrived in the dog-eat-dog social melee of *EVE*.

Everyone seemed energized by this depiction of a previously obscured part of Nell's life and personality. Members were curious to know what her character looked like, what her friends' characters were like and whether she knew where in the country or world her friends lived. Catherine delighted in the image of

Nell as a take-charge swashbuckler. Nell appeared brighter, live-lier, and the others could sense the efficacy in talking about the game. They were reconnecting with the group's ability to help someone feel stronger and healthier and, in so doing, felt it them-selves. All, that is, save one.

"What's up, Lucy?" I asked. She had withdrawn completely from the conversation; she slumped in her chair and stared at the ground.

"Oh, nothing," she said. I could hear the acid in her voice but had no recourse to stop her; after all, I'd invited her to speak. "I just think it's messed up that everyone's cheering on Nell for be-ing a loser with fake internet friends."

Until this point, the group had existed in a protected space that was essential for it to function. Even when there was tension, it was the kind of tension we had all agreed to endure as part of the therapy process; Nell knew as well as anyone, for instance, that if you show up late you are consenting to your lateness being a topic of discussion. But now Lucy had launched a direct attack on Nell by name-calling and dismissing the value of her relation-ships. Lucy was no longer playing with anger or hurt feelings—she was acting abusively.

Each member, including Lucy, recognized that a line had been crossed. Ricardo immediately turned on Lucy, scolding her for her language and attitude; in response she continued staring at the ground. Catherine and a few others looked wide-eyed at me, clearly hoping their de facto leader would take charge to resolve this rupture. I usually aimed to exert my authority as infrequently as possible, seeing myself more as a guide to help members find their ways through conflicts—as in individual therapy, I wanted the group to develop its own agenda for health rather than adhere to mine. When potential space is punctured, however, it is necessary for someone with the credibility to reestablish the boundaries of acceptable behavior—be it a parent, teacher, employer, or therapist—to step in and do so. If members couldn't trust in my ability to protect them from real abuse, they would have no reason to remain in the group at all.

I settled those who were still talking and tried to speak plainly. I acknowledged that what Lucy had said had upset the rest of the group. I also acknowledged that Lucy must have had a reason for saying what she did, which would be important for us to understand as a group. "But first, Lucy, I want to make it clear that the way you expressed yourself just now will not be tolerated here. I could see in your face even as you were speaking that you knew you were lashing out and breaking our mutual agreement to treat one another with decency and respect."

"I was pissed," Lucy said.

"Clearly," I replied. "And I for one want to understand why, as I imagine others do. But this discussion doesn't move forward until you apologize for your behavior. Nell had to own her lateness, you have to own your words."

Lucy said, "Sorry," which felt forced—I had forced it. But it settled the group back into a familiar shape: not yet Bion's "work group," but at least something not at imminent risk of breaking apart. I suggested to Lucy that she may have felt like the group had taken Nell's side.

"I guess," she shrugged. "It just doesn't feel right that we spend so much energy in here trying to cheer you up, Nell, and then forgive you when you're late or don't follow through with the things we talk about . . . and then it turns out the whole time you're having a blast at home on the computer and not telling us!"

"It is strange," Ricardo said to Nell, "that you've never wanted to share with us anything about this game that you love." He opened his mouth as if to say more but stopped, as he saw that Lucy was crying. Everyone turned to her and waited until she was ready to speak.

"I don't have some secret life at home that makes me happy," she said. "What I am in here . . . that's all there is."

The group sat in silence for several moments. Suddenly the preceding twenty minutes since Nell had entered the room felt surreal, like a dream from which we were collectively waking. The sense of urgency that had propelled the group into anxious, asymmetrical forms—Nell versus Lucy, Lucy versus the group—now dissipated and as the fog cleared I felt reminded of how every person in this group was suffering in some way, how frightening and hopeless life could seem, how much each member relied on the group as a beacon of support. How easily those truths could fly out of awareness!

In the weeks to come, various people in the group would weigh in on what had happened that day and reflect on the ways they, too, struggled to share good news in our shared space and at times tolerate the good news of others. The range of members' medical prognoses—from treatable to untreatable but stable, to untreatable and degenerative—was only one of several dimensions that could lead people to struggle with the choice of whether they should express their individuality to the group or try to "fit in" with the group. By acknowledging ways that existing in the group could be difficult there was a paradoxical increase in the closeness and cohesion that everyone felt. It seemed less necessary to skirt sensitive topics that might evoke powerful feelings and easier to identify that abusive moments in the group's past had typically been born from one or more members attempting to avoid or deny such feelings. Nell and Lucy reconciled, openly expressing their care for one another and their regrets over ways in which their actions had hurt the other.

Not all abuse can be prevented and, once perpetrated, therapeutic intervention cannot always be applied to all parties. Particularly in online gaming, when the abuser can be located at great physical distance from the victim, the most appropriate recourse is often for the victim to block the abuser and report the abusive behavior to the game publisher or online platform on which it occurred. Ideally, the abuser will be held accountable and face consequences, such as being suspended or banned from the game. Protecting victims of abuse from further suffering is always the first step, followed by helping them restore a sense of safety and an understanding of what happened. When possible, however, those who engage in abusive behavior can also benefit from not only being reprimanded but also helped to understand their behavior, its impact on others, and its implications about their own suffering.

Understanding the psychological underpinning of online harassment and its impact on those targeted will not only help those at risk of abusing or being abused navigate the densely populated world of online gaming but will promote the development of empathy and social skills that extend to all contexts in which bullying or abuse might occur. Recent inquiries into online harassment have highlighted the fluidity between behavior observed on the internet, in an online game, and in the physical world. A 2016 study by Riot Games, developer of *League of Legends,* demonstrated a high correlation between workplace harassment and "in-game toxicity"—such as frequent use of threatening language—among their employees.[82] The study also found that intervening in one area led to predictable changes in the other, reaffirming the notion that the game was not causing problems in the real world—rather, both in-game and workplace behaviors were the result of a third variable: the employee's emotional state.*

The groups we belong to, physical and virtual, are interlinked, and there is no wrong place to intervene or begin a discussion. Learning to peacefully and respectfully exist in one group—online or in person—will naturally translate to others. You need not be a mental health professional (though finding one is always an option) in order to talk to someone about how they're feeling and why they're behaving the way that they are. Acknowledging a problem opens the door to possible change; ignoring one never does.

---

* As mentioned in Chapter 3's discussion of Gamergate, awareness of a problem is only the first step toward remedying it. Unfortunately, Riot Games apparently did not act quickly to move beyond the awareness raised by their internal study. According to an investigative report published in 2018, the company continued to harbor wide-spread sexism and harassment in the workplace.[83]

Chapter 9

Progression

How can videogames help us face loss and find purpose in life?

I'm afraid that some times
you'll play lonely games too.
Games you can't win
'cause you'll play against you.

—Dr. Seuss, *Oh, The Places You'll Go!*

THE NIGHT BEFORE MY LAST SESSION with Jack, I swore off videogames forever.

My abstention would prove short-lived, but in the moment, I felt furious and bereft and I didn't know what else to do. For a non-trivial number of weeks, I'd poured spare hours into *Demon's Souls*, an action role-playing game that was the talk of the season when it was released. The only problem was that I was terrible at it.

Difficulty in games can be a tricky needle to thread. Designers seek to challenge players without driving them to distraction, rewarding grit and ingenuity while eschewing accusations that the computer is unfairly using its superior speed and processing power to outwit its human counterpart. A common way to impose difficulty is death: If the player does not perform well enough, or fast enough, or focuses too much on one system while overlooking another, her character dies. But even death—the great equalizer of the physical world, final and unambiguous and universal—has its flexibilities in virtual space.

Old coin-op arcade games (and early console videogames inspired by them) often granted the player multiple "lives." As long as there was one or more life left in the bank, death simply meant restarting from a recent checkpoint or even from the exact moment of demise—an opportunity to undo the errors of the past before they became immutable. Once the player was out of lives, however, death meant game over (unless more coins were proffered, of course). Contemporary games have explored myriad other simulations of death and dying, attempting to occupy the space between the brutal reality of life (where death is permanent) and the immortality of fantasy (where death does not exist).

Demon's Souls took a notable approach to this balance, allowing the player a tantalizing but unforgiving opportunity to seek recourse after death. At the start of the game the player would build a character in the vein of other role-playing titles—determining appearance, abilities, and equipment—before sending him out into a grim, medieval world rife with monsters who all seemed to be in varying states of decay. My character was a thief called Sigmund (I have an eye-rolling habit of naming characters after famous psychoanalysts), weak in direct confrontation but agile and lucky, meaning he was more likely than other character types to find useful items in the course of play. Combat represented the lion's share of the *Demon's Souls* system, and engaging in it successfully required deft control over Sigmund: enemies needed to be thoughtfully dodged, parried, and countered, as only a handful of blows could be sufficient to drain his health to zero.

The game presented life and death as dualistic, distinguishing body from spirit. Whenever my character killed a monster, its body would slump to the ground, a useless husk, while an orb of light escaped and was absorbed by Sigmund. This represented the fallen foe's soul, which served as essential currency for me to upgrade Sigmund's abilities and purchase better weapons. Without accruing souls, Sigmund could never grow stronger and I could never hope to move forward in the game.

When Sigmund himself died, he also experienced a metaphysical split, reincarnating at the top of the level (along with any monsters previously slain) as a ghostly version of himself. This spirit form was even frailer than before and robbed of any souls collected prior to death. If I managed to navigate ghost-Sigmund back to the spot where he had been killed, I could reclaim his body and all the souls we'd lost. If, however, Sigmund died again before reentering his body, he would be transported out of the level and all the souls we'd been stocking up would be gone for good.

This is precisely what happened the night before my last session with Jack. After I foolishly allowed Sigmund to be flanked by a couple of spear-wielding skeletons, his spirit folded over in agony, and expletives erupted from my mouth. I leaned back on the couch, perspiring, blood boiling, as the realization sank in that Sigmund and I had been reset to exactly where we were, hours before, when I first sat down to play. I realized, also, that this was more or less where I'd left things the night before—and the night before that. I was *bad* at this, this game about which everyone online seemed to rave. Maybe this medium that I loved—first secretly and more recently with the zeal of professional authority— was leaving me behind.

I looked at Sigmund on the screen, swaying slightly in his idle standing position, holding his measly dagger and shield, ready to start the whole miserable process again. *I've done it all wrong,* I thought: his look, his stats, his equipment. My thief was a runt, a loser, destined to die and die again. If I wanted to keep playing this game I would have to start over, completely, from the beginning. I felt dizzy. This seemed a fate worse than death, Sisyphean labor in which all effort was ultimately for naught; life repeating itself endlessly with nothing learned, nothing gained, nothing to show for it.

My father's voice rang in my ears. "What's the point?"

SAYING GOODBYE TO JACK was difficult, and messy. The process of ending a long-term psychotherapy treatment is always complex, and our ending was made all the more so by the fact that it didn't come about organically. After we had worked together for over two years my training was concluding and I was in the middle of a (somewhat desperate) search for a job. Eventually, I was offered and decided to accept a full-time position at an inpatient psychiatric unit in a city hospital, where I would be unable to continue seeing Jack as an outpatient.

In the months leading up to our last session Jack was preparing to finish college, a major achievement by any standard but particularly remarkable given the struggles he'd been enduring when we first met. His thesis project, unsurprisingly, was making a videogame. We spoke at length about the project, which Jack said was inspired by the John Carpenter film *They Live,* in which a drifter discovers a pair of sunglasses allowing him to see that certain humans—particularly the wealthy elite—are actually aliens in disguise, seeking to manipulate and control the lower classes.

"I like the idea of being able to see different versions of reality by clicking a button to take your sunglasses on or off," Jack told me. "That would work perfectly in a game." I pointed out to him that themes of class and access were long-standing topics from our sessions and had likely stood out to him in the film as ideas to explore in his own work. "That's true," he said, "though I'm dealing with it differently than the movie, which is very violent. The main character in it spends a lot of time fighting and killing the people he sees as aliens. It actually would be easy for me to make my game a shooter, there's a lot of stuff built into the software I'm using that's basically designed for that." Instead of a gun, Jack said, the player in his game would walk around the virtual world—modeled to look like a New York city block—armed with a remote control. "When you click to put on the sunglasses, you see that certain people have televisions for heads and you can use the remote to change their channel and that changes their behavior. Like someone who is blocking a doorway might let you pass through if you tune them right."

Here was a manifestation of the fantasy Jack often held in mind and looked to games to help satisfy: a world in which the actions of others could be understood, predicted, and controlled. Jack acknowledged the appeal of this system, but said he also hoped to introduce complexity in future iterations of the project, such as moral dilemmas (à la *Mass Effect*) born from changing the "channels" of others or forcing the player to negotiate with characters who don't have TV heads and therefore cannot be directly manipulated. "A game where you just make everyone and everything do exactly what you want is really no fun at all," he said. "I want to make something that helps other people feel in control, but also makes them appreciate the fact that not everything can be controlled."

An important part of the end phase of any psychotherapy is openly discussing the patient's progression over time.* The appreciation of change—the very thing one comes to therapy in order to bring about—can be easily lost amid identifying and working through a patient's concerns, even as today's concerns are often built upon the fact that the concerns of last month or last year were resolved in ways that feel stable enough to serve as a foundation for future growth. Reflecting on gains made and shifts across time and space can help to draw conscious attention to how naturally and unconsciously change frequently occurs in psychotherapy. A former supervisor of mine once put it as follows: the process of therapy is like changing the course of a massive ocean liner; you cannot always feel that you have altered your direction, but one day you arrive at a different shore.

By most objective measures the Jack sitting across from me that day looked quite similar to the person I'd met two years earlier. He'd lost a little weight in the interim—the result of a much developed attitude toward diet and exercise—but still gave the visual impression of a scraggly youth, with his overgrown haircut, worn T-shirt, and patch-addled backpack. I recalled our history together: my fear that I was the wrong therapist for the job; our mutual, unspoken inhibition around discussing games that lasted for over a year; his struggles to communicate fundamental emotional experiences without becoming overwhelmed, disoriented, or defensive. Now time had passed, fashion and coif remained unaltered, yet before my eyes was a markedly different Jack—one who cogently and with seemingly

---

* This is not to say assessing progress shouldn't occur in the middle of treatment—it absolutely should—but endings present particular opportunities for reflection.

little conscious effort was discussing how he had synthesized our work deeply enough that his insights could be reconstituted as a creative product.

I felt, in a word, proud—and I told him as much.

"Thank you," he said, his face flushing slightly. "It is hard to remember sometimes where I was at a year ago, let alone two years ago. It's . . . I've come a long way."

WHILE CELEBRATING THE VALUE of a relationship is a necessary part of addressing separation, it is also insufficient. Separation also involves loss, which is complex and bittersweet, and the sadness of ending must be acknowledged alongside the joy of what came before it. No goodbye party, graduation, or funeral feels complete without laughter *and* tears. For all the attention Jack and I paid to patting one another on the back, validating our work and our relationship, we avoided in equal measure talking about why we were so invested in looking back: because, looking forward, we would no longer be together.

Some of our avoidance was couched in flimsy rationalization. For a stretch of time, as my job prospects were up in the air, I dangled the notion that we might continue working together in a private setting. This was, in retrospect, pure denial. I had no concrete plans to open a private practice at such a nascent phase of my postdoctoral career; I was far too distracted with the obligations of finishing my degree and seeking gainful employment to even consider that option seriously. Jack was happy to take my bait, of course—how was he to know the veracity of my purported plans?—and so we colluded in the idea that separation could be discussed later because, hey, maybe at the end of the day we wouldn't need to separate at all. I met weekly at this time with a supervisor who consulted on my treatment with Jack and she was starting to sound like a broken record.

"You need to talk about ending," she'd say. "You need to put words to the fact that you're leaving, that it is a loss for both of you. Losses need time and language to be mourned."

"Yes," I would reply. "You're right. I'll talk with him about it." And I wouldn't.

Meanwhile, at home I was torturing myself with *Demon's Souls*. You'd be excused for thinking that, given all the time I'd devoted to considering the psychological meaning of videogames over the preceding years, I might have stopped to reflect on why, exactly, I returned night after night to a game I kept failing at, felt inept at—indeed, had begun to hate playing. But periods of high stress have a way of clicking us back into familiar grooves and obscuring, if temporarily, more recently acquired perspectives.

My unpleasant relationship with *Demon's Souls* was, I think, an unconscious attempt to absolve myself of the guilt of leaving Jack, while simultaneously engaging in an act of self-flagellation. In the course of my training I had parted ways with many patients, often due to the artificial circumstance of a trainee moving to a new clinic or hospital. But Jack and I had a unique history in my professional experience up to that point, even if it was a history of which he was not fully aware: I had been assigned to work with Jack—hand-picked—because of what others saw as my unique potential to understand him. Games had, in a sense, brought us together, bonded us, helped facilitate the changes in Jack's life that we were now celebrating. More insidiously, they also bred in me a fierce protectiveness, a feeling that no one but I could have guided Jack through the chaos and darkness of his inner and outer worlds. And now I was abandoning him.

Had I internalized Jack's unspoken fear of abandonment? Perhaps. But I was also on some level aware that I was walking away from a relationship in which I had placed a great deal of meaning. While it is true that no one else could have had precisely the same relationship and treatment that Jack and I created together—just as all relationships are defined in part by the uniqueness of their individual members—I had for my own sense of purpose and self-esteem cast myself as a kind of savior: an indispensable, irreplaceable fixture of Jack's life. The transition out of graduate school and into the workforce, and the stress of finding a job, surely contributed to my feverish need to see myself this way. Ironically, it also fed my reluctance to talk openly with Jack about my role in his life and what it would be like to say goodbye. I had backed myself into an anxious corner: I needed to feel that Jack needed me, yet I also had to go. I think I would have been as afraid to hear him say that he couldn't bear to go on without me as to hear him say that he could.

So, I played *Demon's Souls*, a corrosive nightly ritual in which I seemed to be trying to prove to myself, one death at a time, that I had outgrown games—or they had outgrown me—and that I no longer had anything valuable to contribute to that world and those who participated in it. If my relationship with games was over, my relationship with Jack wouldn't have much left to stand on, at least in the bleary half-logic of my unconscious mind. I would have nothing to feel bad about and he wouldn't really miss me, anyway. It was an attempt at mourning that was actually a kind of unmourning, denying the loss and the emotions that make loss painful. I was participating in a cycle reminiscent of one you may recall that Tim from the television program *Spaced* was locked in while trying to cope with a break-up. He drowned Lara

Croft, only for her to resurrect, unharmed, primed for redrowning. Tension and release, tension and release. The process helped him divert his overwhelming feelings to a point of catharsis, but provided no understanding, no way out of the closed loop. *Tomb Raider 3* never forced Tim to confront the fact that, as Jack said, "not everything can be controlled." Loss is part of life, but if the pain of it seems too great to bear we run from it, deny that it is real, refuse to see it as meaningful. As a result, we paradoxically become defined by the loss—our thoughts, feelings, and actions dictated by the need to keep the pain of it at bay.

Mourning is a progression, a working through; denying that such progression is possible is not mourning but despair, not sadness but a kind of depression.* I toiled for hours on *Demon's Souls,* hacking through enough monsters to ensure progression, some forward movement out of the grind, the muck and mire, only to lose myself once again, body and spirit, and revert. Playing the game felt impossible and therefore could serve as a repository for all my frustrated and conflicted feelings, my guilt and self-reproach—but it couldn't offer me a way through. Really, I shouldn't have purchased *Demon's Souls* in the first place. All its press centered on the punishing difficulty level and I'd never regarded myself as the most adroit of players. I typically favored slower games focused on narrative or puzzles over twitch-muscle dexterity. Yet I had blocked out this basic understanding of my taste and ability, equating the demands of *Demon's Souls* with a global standard on the state of games and my place within it.

---

* Freud, after whom I named my *Demon's Souls* character, drew this distinction in his 1917 essay "Mourning and Melancholia."[84] Ernest Becker made a similar connection between depression and refusing to accept loss in his landmark 1973 book *The Denial of Death.*[85]

Since I was bad at this one, I should probably just abandon this lifelong passion of mine altogether.

Such an extreme conclusion partially served as a means to ignore the ambivalence I felt over whether or not to play the game that Jack had made for his thesis project. As we approached our final session he suggested that he might bring his laptop in one day so that I could see it for myself. I felt uneasy about spending one of our last hours together staring at a computer screen while Jack, in turn, stared at me, and I was even more uncomfortable about being in a position to give a definitive opinion on something Jack had created. I told him that if it were possible for him to send the game to me I would play it on my own time. He agreed but appeared visibly disappointed. Internally, I justified my decision through my abject failure at playing *Demon's Souls:* I was so off the pulse of contemporary games that my opinion of Jack's work wouldn't be worth much to him, even if he didn't know it yet.

I would probably make the same call today in terms of not actually playing a game in session (just as I would also not be likely to read a story or listen to a song brought in by a patient during a session), but my greatest regret during the closing weeks of working with Jack was that I didn't speak to him honestly about my thought process. Today, I would talk about why I didn't play the game: He and I needed to give language to our feelings, the mixture of sadness, anger, love, and accomplishment that intermingled around our parting. Offering to bring in his game was a gesture from Jack, a farewell gift, one that I bungled by neither accepting nor explaining that my lack of acceptance was not a rejection, but rather an acknowledgment that no gift could hide the fact that Jack and I would both have to find ways to mourn the loss of the other.

I remember few details from my last session with Jack and, if I took any private notes beyond the clinic's requisite documentation, they were subsequently destroyed. The hour had a surreal feel about it. Perhaps we both still held on to a fantasy that we would resume working together again someday soon—that this wasn't really an ending. We said "Goodbye." He never sent his game.

In the months following I thought of him often; I missed him. Our work had been meaningful to me and I felt conflicted about turning down the opportunity to experience a digital world of his creation. I had chosen to move on from Jack, which was painful in and of itself, and the pain was compounded by the fact that I now found myself at a job that I absolutely hated.

As HUMAN BEINGS we are uniquely blessed and cursed with the ability to contemplate death. Even more, we can abstract it: Beyond literal, physical death we speak often of being spiritually deadened or reborn; we declare that a former friend or lover, following some betrayal, is now "dead" to us. Corporeal death is in fact only one extreme of many points along a continuum of loss, any and all of which we have the capacity to reflect on, deal with or flee. This capacity has, over the course of our species' development, made us into instinctive meaning-makers: we seek purpose in our lives in an effort to grapple with the unanswerable question of why we are here and the awareness that someday we and those we love—will not be. The flip side of this coin is that we are also prone to existential despair and depression if our lives feel empty or meaningless.

My new position—as a staff psychologist on an inpatient psychiatric unit in a hospital within a poor, urban neighborhood—

felt nothing short of Kafkaesque. I spent much of my day sitting in a tiny, windowless office filling out paperwork for patients with whom I barely had time to speak. I was tasked with case management and social-work duties for which I had little to no training and was told by supervisors in no uncertain terms that, compared to these duties, doing psychotherapy with my patients should be low on my priority list. I had to fight hard to be allotted time to run one or two therapy groups per week, citing state regulations to the unit chief, in language that fell just shy of a direct threat to report what I saw as questionable management ethics.

I had thought over the past several years of my professional training that I had developed a good sense of the plight of the mentally ill and impoverished and the way systems often fail to meet those people's basic needs. At times these systems can even be set up to prevent them from getting well. But my new hospital operated on a whole different level—an eye-opening, soul-crushing level. If I can say I learned anything from working there it would be within the domain of how to exploit destitute individuals for profit out of an assumption that no one is watching—and that if anyone is watching they probably don't care.

Within this grisly milieu I questioned the value of the work I was doing: scrambling to shore up patients in the throes of acute phases of severe mental illness before sending them back out to a community with more predatory agencies than genuinely helpful ones, only to see them return to the hospital within weeks, the same or worse off than when I had discharged them. No one cared about my point of view as a psychologist or my ideas about how to improve the unit. Most were too busy scrambling around themselves, as they were also placed in positions that stretched their professional competency to a breaking point (the nursing staff, for instance, had no special training in working with psychiatric patients, which should have been standard practice). There was one other psychologist working alongside me and he and I forged a friendship built on mutual resentment of our circumstances, easing our daily frustrations through gossip and bitter trash-talking of coworkers and bosses. I grew more caustic, less curious. Friends noticed. My wife was supportive but admitted that she felt confused and paralyzed: She had never seen me so adrift.

Then, in an effort to occupy myself in my spare time, I did something I had never done before: I made a videogame. It was nothing fancy. All text—like Crowther and Woods's *Adventure* and the games it inspired, which in turn inspired the games that my father and I played together on our old IBM—and made with minimal coding using a free development tool called Twine.* I titled it *Progression,* a term that in videogames usually denotes a linear movement from first-level novice to final-boss expert, but in psychotherapy can refer to a much more nebulous transition from one state of being to another.

At least one of the transitions I was exploring was taking me from games-player to creator. This possibility had long appealed to me and also held a firm place in the broader history of games. Since the early 1980s—essentially the dawn of widely available videogames—developers had experimented with including, alongside their finished products, tools that players could use to construct their own additions and modifications to a title. Some "level editors" were made for ease of use, allowing anyone

---

* Twine is the same platform, incidentally, that Zoe Quinn used to make *Depression Quest,* discussed in Chapter 3. The software and a directory of games created with it can be found at twinery.org.

with time and interest to try their hand at game design within the narrow confines of the game for which the editor was built. Others demanded more technical prowess but in exchange gave player-creators extensive reign over what they could make, using existing assets and systems from the original game. In some instances, fan-derived "mods" of commercial titles went on to become blockbusters in their own rights.* Increasingly, contemporary games bake creation right into the primary play experience: the titanic popularity of *Minecraft,* as previously discussed, was rooted in the freedom it granted players to build and share things of their own design. Tools like Twine and the ease of online distribution have made it possible for people to make and release homemade games that decades ago would have required large teams and significant financial backing to achieve.

It shouldn't be surprising that there is substantial overlap between the desire to play and the desire to create. At its most universal, the relationship between a player and a game is about entering another's world—linked to but separate from our own—and exploring its potential and one's potential within it. A pull toward being the one who makes the world that *others* might explore represents a natural curiosity; to feel what it's like to be on the other side of a relationship. In the world of psychotherapy training this kind of curiosity is not only encouraged but often required: Many graduate programs consider going through therapy as a patient to be a prerequisite to earning one's degree. The rationale is not only that therapists need to address their own

---

* *Counter-Strike,* a complete repurposing of the engine powering the popular 1998 game *Half-Life,* is the most cited example of this phenomenon. Its amateur creators were subsequently hired by *Half-Life*'s developer, and *Counter-Strike* remains a venerable commercial franchise.

inner struggles before attempting to address those of others but, to an even greater extent, that in order to be an effective and empathic therapist one ought to have some sense of what it feels like to be a patient.

Progression was about two brothers descending an ancient structure together, seeking some unknown reward at its depths.* Small portions of text would be displayed to the player, like a short story told in the second person and revealed a few paragraphs at a time. Each passage contained hyperlinks carrying some implication about how the player might drive the story forward, though exactly how was often left opaque. The first time playing through would feel to most like stabbing in the dark, arbitrarily clicking links without any real sense of agency or a coherent system. But I was OK with that because, before long, the player would end up selecting a path that resulted in her untimely demise. The game would start again, exactly as before, though the player might notice that her steadily accruing "experience points" had not reset[†] and furthermore she was now armed with her memory of what she had attempted previously and where it had led her. The game thus invited the player to repeat her journey downward in iterative loops—dying and resurrecting, trying new options and learning from mistakes—before an understanding of who their character was and what they were really seeking became clearer.

During the development process, I never consciously thought that this was a way to hold on to my relationship with Jack—by building a game like the ones that had bonded us, like the one

---

* Interested readers can play it for free at philome.la/alexmkriss/progression/play

† Creating this mechanic may, in part, have represented my direct act of defying *Demon's Souls,* in which the player's "experience" (measured in souls) was always at risk of evaporating.

he had made, the one I had declined to play. I never consciously thought about the fact that I was applying all my adult faculties toward creating something that looked like a game from my childhood, a game my father could understand. I didn't even think about how forcing the player to endure a seemingly endless life-death cycle while only gradually eking out some sense of movement could be a way of working through the deadening cycle that I endured every day at work. I just made the thing and then put it online for the world to play or ignore.

The response was overwhelming. By the standards of the professional games industry, public interest would have been considered paltry, but as someone emerging grey and defeated from a windowless room every day at five o'clock, the fact that thousands of people opted to spend time in my little world felt like a blast of fresh ocean air. Not only did friends and strangers play it, but they puzzled over it, explored and tested its depths and branching pathways—a couple of people even posted hint guides and elaborate theories about the game's meaning on online message boards, just as I had with *Silent Hill 2* and other major games of my life.

I'm not naive: I would have left my job in short order, no matter what. But the process of making and sharing a game reminded me in a visceral way that directly connecting with other people and sharing meaningful experiences with them was incredibly important to me—and incredibly absent from my current position. This reminder helped me to envision that my next step didn't have to be moving from one hospital to another, from a system I detested to one about which I might hope to feel, at best, ambivalent. Very quickly, the notion of private practice, a setting in which there would be no bureaucracy between myself and the people I was trying to help, went from the vague impossibility it had seemed to be when I parted with Jack to appearing as something vital, something I wanted to pursue in spite of the risks. My job had become an all-too-real manifestation of my relationship with *Demon's Souls:* an interminable convolution with no purpose; a punishment I resented and yet on some level felt I deserved. *Progression,* then, served as a vehicle for actual mourning: not just a static loop but a kind of movement, a working through. It was a trial run for pushing myself in a new direction, of choosing to confront my despair rather than be consumed by it—all within the safety of the game-space that I had long relied upon to process and explore parts of myself and my experience.

The game concluded, ambiguously, with the player reaching the bottom of the dungeon and being given the choice to forgive who she finds there—possibly her father, another version of herself, or a chimera of past trauma (all these interpretations were suggested by players online)—or destroy him and take his place in that darkest of depths. Forgiveness is not uncomplicated, however: it involves saying "Goodbye" to the person waiting at the bottom, whoever he may be, and beginning the long, slow journey back to the surface.

Creating *Progression* was not only my way of saying goodbye to Jack, but of forgiving myself for the errors I felt I had made. Through it I gave myself permission to learn from my mistakes, climb back out, and continue to pursue a meaningful life.

Games offer many ways to consider the terror of death and the sorrow of loss from the impermanent vantage point of the virtual: the death–rebirth cycle of the player's character puts us through the rigors of dying while evading death's finality; the deaths of in-game enemies and allies connect us to a wide range of emotions around loss, from the socially acceptable ones like sadness and anger to more taboo feelings like relief and joy; once a beloved game is mastered, shelving it is in and of itself a separation and loss that reminds the player that something has been accomplished, but also that time has marched on and feelings once felt have now passed. Even more importantly, games can serve as a staging post for coping with the existential threat that death and loss evoke that nagging notion that life's transience begs the question of whether it's worth anything at all. At times when players—or creators—are struggling to find purpose elsewhere in their lives, the potential of games—and the act of sharing them with others can prove invaluable.

I have no idea if Jack has ever stumbled across my game online. It is possible and perhaps ultimately inconsequential. I didn't make it for him, though he is inextricably a part of it. At the very least, I'd like to think that if he were to play it, he would understand.

Chapter 10

Next-Gen

What is the future of our lives with videogames?

The world should take note: not everything is getting worse.

—Ian McEwan, *Saturday*

NOT LONG AGO, a nineteen-year-old named Levi came to see me with a most unusual problem: He couldn't play videogames anymore.

The issue was more urgent for him than it would be for most. Levi was a high-ranking e-sports athlete, which meant that playing games was his chief source of income. But after a series of anxiety attacks he had begun to withdraw from tournaments and, eventually, couldn't even bring himself to practice in the privacy of his home.

Levi appeared affable sitting across from me, with a gentle disposition and wide, searching eyes. He struck me as a curious child and a wise old man all at once, an impression that was likely influenced by his own report of feeling lost somewhere between adolescence and adulthood. After graduating high school, one and a half years earlier, Levi had devoted himself entirely to his e-sports career—until two months before I met him, when he abruptly dropped out of competitive play. Since then, Levi said, he spent most of his time at home not knowing what to do with him- self. He had moved back in with his parents after over a year of financial independence; e-sports reporters had started throwing around terms like "indefinite hiatus" in speculative online articles. Life felt, in his words, "unreal."

"If I can't get over this and start playing again, I don't know what's going to happen," he told me. "Which sounds so weird to say. Not only because I've never had this kind of anxiety before, but because when I was a kid this wasn't a thing. This wasn't a problem a person could have."

Levi was not so young and wide-eyed that he believed anxiety to be newly invented. What he meant was that even a few years earlier—as a high-school student uninterested in academics and enamored of games—the field of e-sports had been so nascent that it had never occurred to him that he could make a living do- ing the thing he loved.* In sessions he marveled repeatedly over the idea that he'd made manifest a career path that as a child ex- isted purely in fantasy ("People will pay me to play videogames!"), with no indication that it would ever be possible. Today, it was not only a possibility but Levi's reality, yet his body seemed to be rejecting that very fact.

The problem itself was not so novel, despite Levi's insistence that his "e-sports injury," as he sometimes referred to his anxiety, was the first of its kind. (He pointed to the dearth of Google search results on the subject as evidence of his condition's sin-

---

* Levi's depiction of the sudden emergence of professional gaming was not the misperception of an uninformed teenager. The industry's rise has been as remarkable for its speed as its scope (three of the major gaming markets— North America, China, and South Korea—represent less than two-thirds of global e-sports revenue combined). Total revenue in 2016 was estimated at around $500 million and just two years later that figure had nearly doubled—putting e-sports on the cusp of being a billion-dollar industry.[86]

gularity.) Here was a young person transitioning from one phase of life to another—the confinement and safety of school-age existence to the terrifying, liberating open field of being a grown-up—paralyzed by the experience of dragging his unfettered fantasies into the drudgery of daily life. One could easily imagine a similar scenario with a more traditional sports athlete, in which he or she could no longer effectively shoot a basketball or swing a bat.

But traditional sports was not Levi's world. To understand his dilemma in full required an appreciation of the player–game relationship detailed in the preceding chapters: the intersection of system and character; the use of the game world as a potential space; the way Levi's idiosyncratic approach to play reflected a deeper psychological dynamic. My adolescence had been marked by a stigma and suspicion surrounding games—I hid or minimized them with friends and family, I avoided talking about them in therapy and I carried that shame forward into my adulthood and early clinical career. Now, however, with Levi, I had the benefit of my preceding years of analyzing games and treating players and he could in turn benefit from my growth as a clinician and human being.

He hadn't just arrived on my doorstep by chance, of course. Levi was referred to me by a colleague who had met him once for a consultation and felt uneasy about her ability to help.

"Games are clearly so important to this young man and to his presenting problem," she told me over the phone. "It feels too far outside any space I really know about. I think he ought to see someone who understands games and can talk to him with more credibility than I can about what they might mean to him."*

---

* While I don't think a therapist needs to be an expert in every area of a patient's life in order for treatment to be effective, a base of knowledge—and a willingness to learn more, as relevant to the case—is sometimes essential, especially if the area in question covers a large part of why the patient is coming to therapy.

Hand on heart, it didn't occur to me until I started writing this book that this was the same colleague who first called Jack a "gamer kid." We had remained close in the intervening years and had shared so many personal and professional experiences since that staff meeting that I no longer automatically associated her with it. The shift, on reflection, was significant: from a dismissive pigeonholing of Jack to a thoughtful assessment that Levi's relationship with games deserved attention and expertise. Recently, I asked for her thoughts on this change—what had catalyzed it? A natural evolution as a clinician? Direct exposure to games through her friendship with me? A sea change in how games are viewed by the public in general?

She shrugged and said, "Probably a bit of everything. We're all figuring this out as we go, right? Isn't that why we call it 'practice'?"

LEVI COMPETED IN ONE-ON-ONE fighting games, in which two players set their characters on one another in a brawl to the death (or at least a knockout). In some ways it's a more intense form of competition than team-based e-sports, both in terms of the demands during play—if you lose there's no one else to blame—and outside of it, as an e-sports celebrity. E-sports teams take their lead from established sports franchises for marketing and promotional tactics: developer and publisher Activision Blizzard has gone so far as to assign teams associated with their smash-hit *Overwatch* to specific cities in order to generate local fan bases and rivalries. But Levi's circuit was more akin to boxing: Rising in stature seemed to be as dependent on cultivating a larger-than-life personality as his actual in-game performance. Even more, there was clear pressure for Levi and his fellow competitors to stoke (or pretend to stoke) personal beefs with one another in order to infuse matches with narratives of vengeance and score-settling when they otherwise might not hold much interest for fans. The greater the feud, the greater the publicity; the greater the publicity, the greater the viewership; the greater the viewership, the greater the sponsorship deals.

One of the beefs in which Levi was embroiled had escalated over the course of months, and he saw it as a primary source of his debilitating anxiety.

"This guy . . . I think he really hates me or something," Levi said. "He's not playing around."

His choice of words was astute. The rivalry Levi spoke of did not feel playful at all, but heavy and consequential. Much of his experience of the professional world in general since leaving high school could be described in this way: While Levi's life still revolved around games, games no longer felt like *play*.

I asked Levi to tell me more about what drew him to the games he played competitively—which notably were the only games he ever played—and how he viewed himself within the e-sports community. He answered with one word: "Perfectionist." He went on to say that since long before his professional status, he had gravitated toward characters that he and others categorized as "glass cannons." In the context of fighting games, these characters were defined by being extremely powerful if handled with near-perfect precision—with the emphasis on "perfect." It would be difficult to overstate the minute, frame-by-frame level of scrutiny that players of Levi's caliber imposed on themselves when honing their skills. A glass cannon, properly harnessed, had the potential to deal more damage with greater speed than any other character in the game, but it was a double-edged sword. As the "glass" portion of the name suggests, the power of Levi's preferred characters was offset by their exceptional vulnerability. In the wake of the slightest player error this would expose itself and they could be swiftly shattered by a well-timed counterattack.

Levi felt invigorated by this challenge: He saw the game world as a space where, through hard work and dedication, objective perfection could be achieved. If the smallest misstep led to failure, success meant that he had performed flawlessly; the most demanding characters yielded the greatest satisfaction upon mastery. Levi went so far as to say that, to his mind, there were no other "real" characters than the glass cannon types—the rest were "just fluff" for less dedicated or talented players.

Of course, the stakes of playing a glass cannon were tempered always by the artifice of game-space, where the consequence of imperfection was contained. A lost match was a lost match; at worst causing a surge of anger, at best motivating Levi to practice and improve. As Levi transitioned from amateur enthusiast to e-sports celebrity, however, the familiar containment no longer held. Imperfect play now carried real-world fallout. Now a lost match was more than a lost match, but also a loss of money and a possible loss of standing in future tournaments. The purity of his gaming self began to feel spoiled by the emotional and financial complexity associated with being a professional player. Games could no longer only be about achieving nirvana in a bounded virtual world—they now also carried the burden of earning a living, attracting sponsors and maintaining well-publicized rivalries with other players. What had once been Levi's method of alleviating anxiety and avoiding life's traumatic potential was now the source of his trouble. The need to play perfectly became confused with a panicked sense of needing to *live* perfectly, a bar that Levi felt ill-equipped to meet—who wouldn't? Under such conditions, there was no room for the experimentation of play, the freedom it offered of trial-and-error learning, the adoption of multiple roles and selves or the defiance of the very laws of space and time.

Once Levi and I had framed his anxiety in this way, our work essentially became the process of helping him relearn to play. The job of e-sports needed to be disentangled in Levi's mind from his personal connection to games and the private, emotional meaning they brought to him. Playing a game didn't have to adhere to a singular philosophy anymore; the role that games occupied in Levi's childhood could be modified and expanded to accommodate the new demands of his adult life. The unambiguous pursuit of perfection that glass cannons represented had made sense to Levi as a teenager feeling unremarkable in school and social circles. But now his needs had changed: he was publicly regarded as quite remarkable in the e-sports world and subsequently felt desperate for some low-pressure respite. He started testing out other characters at home that he knew he would never use in a tournament setting—as well as playing games he had no intention of publicly competing in—and reported finding great satisfaction in play that stood apart from his hectic professional life. Though how, and what, he played had changed, his experience of play was reconnecting him with something deeply familiar: the feelings of safety and sanctity that had made games so important to him in the first place.

The problems of adulthood didn't evaporate—no game or therapy holds such power—but carving out space to truly play helped Levi see these problems as less overwhelming. The rivalries and sponsorships of e-sports still felt stressful and onerous, but Levi began to feel more solidly able to manage them—a feeling bolstered, in part, by his allowing himself to consider quitting e-sports if he ultimately decided it didn't suit him.

"I'm realizing I don't *have* to do this," he said. "It doesn't mean I won't still love games, or still see the friends I've made through competing. But all these things don't have to go together. I can change them if I want to. I'll still be me."

As may be self-evident at this point, the language I develop with patients often revolves in some way around the boundaries between fantasy and reality, inside and outside. Some, like Jack, need help erecting those borders so that they can more easily distinguish between different states; others, like Levi, benefit from reminders that borders that were once rigid and fixed can be made flexible as circumstances and life change. The construction and reconstruction of these essential boundaries hinges on my ability to meet others at the intersection of fantasy and reality, where we as individuals come into contact with the rest of the world. That contact, ideally, is play: experiencing our thoughts and feelings through interaction with someone or something else is play; contemplating and discussing the possibility of change is play. A "videogame" may mean many things to many people—inscrutable technology, beloved pastime, soother, torturer, fantasy of power, proof of inadequacy, mind-numbing time-suck, social gathering point—but play is universal. We are all entitled to play. We need to play in order to fully discover and live as ourselves.

SOMETIMES I FANTASIZE ABOUT a day when my son will look up at me and ask what it was like to live in a world without *Minecraft*. The increasing normality of growing up inside virtual worlds will inevitably affect development and mental health treatment for the next generation, and imagining life without games will become as dizzying a mental exercise as imagining life without the internet or cars. Already games have a reactionary corner carved out for them in the psychopathology market: They have a dedicated diagnosis thanks to the World Health Organization, and specialized treatment centers of unclear merit exist and will continue to spring up around the globe. But games are also now being considered for their potential to address psychological and social problems. Virtual simulations have or are being developed to help first responders prepare to deal with worst-case (but all too common) scenarios like school shootings,[87] and a new wave of research is suggesting that games can be a helpful component of treating post-traumatic stress disorder in active-duty soldiers and veterans.[88] Let the irony not be lost that, in those latter two examples, people are turning to videogames in hopes of reducing the destructive consequences of violence—a sharp turn from the decades-long tendency to blame games for causing such consequences.

Outside of clinical and professional settings—that is, in the fray of regular life—children depend on videogames more and more as a means of exploring the social and emotional aspects of being human. Technologists might argue that new media like videogames can only make us brighter, stronger, faster—that "new" is synonymous with a kind of linear progress. This is not really the case. Alarmists, conversely, have long said that games are the seed of antisocial behavior in our civilization. This is also untrue—such behavior is hardly new to the human condition.

I am not immune to such polarities when something new and opaque arrives on the scene. I still bristle when I see photos of my young niece warped by a Snapchat filter to give her sparkling, cartoonish eyes, whiskers, and bunny ears. What is viewing herself through this distorted lens doing to her sense of self and her sense of how others see her? It's another black box: I don't fully understand the technology or what it means to my niece, so my fears run wild about the dark and twisting transactions that might be taking place unseen between them. Friends and colleagues (far hipper than me) tell me that Snapchat filters can offer a kind of post-human freedom, the ability to quickly and compellingly transcend our physical appearance with a few taps on a touchscreen. Maybe I'm a worrywart; maybe they're naive. Certainly, my anxiety and their enthusiasm both move faster than science does—good science, at least, founded on sound, responsible methods intended to help us understand new phenomena rather than put a premature label on some emergent source of cultural anxiety. In the meantime, we must learn to slow ourselves down, regard claims of quick fixes and definitive proof with suspicion and take care of one another.

I worry about what black boxes my son will encounter as he grows up and how I will deal with them. Through judgment and dismissal? Blind faith and acceptance? My entire life, to some extent, has been a journey to find where videogames lie between these extremes: from the earliest days of playing alongside my father, through my work with Jack and into the present day. The player–game relationship is not one of "doer" and "done to" but something mutual, in which both parties collaborate to build an experience—and as such, both hold a measure of responsibility for that experience. How a game functions and what kind of message it is trying to convey are important, but no more important than the needs, fears, and dynamics—both conscious and unconscious—that reside within any given player.

Understanding videogames of the past, present, and future is therefore not about deciding whether they are good or bad, helpful or harmful, mark of salvation or horseman of the apocalypse. Games are here and growing; they are a way for us to learn more about who we are or make contact with parts of ourselves we didn't know existed. The game is an open world, a place of promise and ambiguity that may mean little on its own but can mean a great deal when bonded with the player. This meaning may be of vital significance to someone going through any number of the problems and transitions we all face in life, and it is our responsibility as parents, therapists, teachers, partners, and friends to remain open to what that meaning might be and not allow stigma and confusion to stifle genuine curiosity. If we are able to remain open to the new medium of games, the potential is effectively limitless. By letting us literally play around with who we are and who we could be, games invite us into a deeper understanding of ourselves, our friends and families, and our broader communities.

If you love someone who plays games—or you love someone who struggles to understand why *you* play games—and I can leave you with no other message, let it be this: Talk to each other about it! Games don't bite and neither does an open conversation about thoughts and feelings. Understanding is not difficult, but *wanting* to understand can be, and to a surprising degree. Wanting to understand requires that we be curious about the things we don't know and flexible enough to question the things we think we do know. It requires that we care more about learning than holding on to a rigid worldview. And it requires that when looking at others, we are open to looking at ourselves.

Acknowledgments

I am grateful to my wonderful agents at the Science Factory, especially Tisse Takagi who held my hand assuredly during the development of this book's proposal. My friend Anne Rumberger was also instrumental in encouraging me to pursue this project in the first place and consulted on early proposal drafts. Andrew McAleer and the UK team at Robinson took a chance on me as a first-time author, for which I will be forever thankful, and Batya Rosenblum and everyone at The Experiment worked tirelessly to bring the book back home to North America.

From September 2014 to November 2016 I wrote periodically for the now-defunct website and print magazine *Kill Screen*. I am indebted to that publication—and particularly to editors Clayton Purdom and Chris Priestman—for allowing me a space to develop and share various ideas about the psychology of playing games, a few of which made their way into this book in a revised form. A very early version of my Chapter 1 exploration of *Silent Hill 2* appeared on the Kill Screen website on October 31, 2014, in an article titled, "*Silent Hill 2*'s Endings Aren't What You Want, But What You Deserve." The Chapter 2 section about Tim from *Spaced*'s relationship with *Tomb Raider 3* was adapted from part of an article called "Killing Lara Croft," originally published on the Kill Screen website on July 20, 2015. A version of the Chapter 5 section on my treatment with Cole first appeared as a feature titled "Do Games Desensitize Us?" in issue ten of *Kill Screen,* published in November 2016.

The following supervisors directly impacted my clinical thinking and practice—whether we ever spoke explicitly about videogames or not, these individuals shaped me as a psychologist and by extension my representation of the psychotherapy process in this book: Christopher Christian, Ali Khadivi, Mark Kuras, Jeremy Safran, Herbert Schlesinger, Lauryn Schmerl, David Shapiro, and Ariela Vasserman.

Thanks to my *D&D* crew—Molly Auerbach, Joanna Beer, Eric Monte, and David Sims—for obvious reasons.

Without the love and support of Dawn Kriss, my wife and best friend, I wouldn't be able to write a word. This book exists because of her.

Lastly, I am thankful to my patients, past and present, for granting me the extraordinary privilege of knowing them, learning from them, and helping them to heal and grow.

Notes

Chapter 1

1. *The Black Cauldron,* developed and published by Sierra On-Line, 1986.
2. *The Legend of Kyrandia,* developed by Westwood Studios, published by Virgin Games, 1992.
3. *Ibid.*
4. Chris Morris, "Goodbye *Myst.* Hello *Sims,*" *CNN Money,* March 28, 2002, money. cnn.com/2002/03/27/commentary/game_over/ column_gaming.
5. Critical Path, "Toby Gard—Playing A Female Character," YouTube, January 11, 2017, youtube.com/watch?v=8PyBEmj7StQ.
6. *Silent Hill 2,* developed by Team Silent, published by Konami, 2001.
7. *Ibid.*
8. *Ibid.*
9. *Ibid.*
10. *Ibid.*

Chapter 2

11. *Legend of Zelda: Ocarina of Time* speed-run information, accessed November 18, 2019, speedrun.com/oot/run/y215p47z.
12. Khurram Imtiaz, "*Fallout 4* World Map Compared With *Fallout 3,* Takes Eleven Minutes To Traverse In Game," GearNuke, November 4, 2015, gearnuke.com/ fallout-4-world-map-comparedfallout-3-takes-11 -minutestraverse-game.

13. "Why do people like Mario?," GameSpot, accessed June 22, 2018, gamespot.com/forums/nintendofan-club-1000001/ why-dopeople-like-mario-33371686.

14. Nathan Grayson, "*Hellblade* Is Great Because It's Frustrating," Kotaku, August 8, 2017, kotaku.com/ hellblade-is-great-becauseit-s-frustrating-1797654673.

15. Critical Path, "Toby Gard—Playing A Female Character," YouTube, January 11, 2017, youtube.com/watch?v=8PyBEmj7StQ.

16. *Spaced*, "Battles," episode four. Directed by Edgar Wright, written by Jessica Stevenson and Simon Pegg. Channel 4, October 15, 1999.

Chapter 3

17. Tristan Donovan, *Replay: The History of Videogames* (Lewes, East Sussex: Yellow Ant, 2010), pp. 4–5.

18. Sigmund Freud, "Introductory Lectures on Psycho-Analysis," in *The Standard Edition of the Complete Psychological Works of Sigmund Freud, Volume XVI (1916–1917): Introductory Lectures on Psycho-Analysis (Part III)* (1917), pp. 241–463, PEP Web.

19. Lucas Peterson, "What Tech Tools Frequent Travelers Should Always Pack," *The New York Times*, December 6, 2017, nytimes .com/2017/12/06/technology/personaltech/tech-tools-travel.html.

20. Heather Braga, "46 Gifts For Gamers That Will Make You Player One In Their Eyes," BuzzFeed, December 14, 2018, buzzfeed .com/hbraga/gifts-for-gamers.

21. Donovan, *Replay*, p. 5.

22. Dennis G. Jerz, "Somewhere Nearby Is Colossal Cave: Examining Will Crowther's Original *Adventure* in Code and in Kentucky," *Digital Humanities Quarterly* 1, no. 2 (2007), digitalhumanities .org/dhq/vol/001/2/000009/000009.html.

23. Katie Hatner and Matthew Lyon, *Where Wizards Stay Up Late: The Origins of the Internet* (New York: Touchstone, 1998), p. 112.

24. Jerz, "Colossal Cave."

25. *Ibid.*

26. *Ibid.*

27. *Ibid.*

28. Donovan, *Replay*, p. 51.

29. *Ibid.*, p. 51.

30. Jon Peterson, *Playing at the World* (San Diego, California: Unreason, 2012), pp. 114–15.

31. Jerz, "Colossal Cave."

32. Steven L. Kent, *The Ultimate History of Videogames* (New York: Three Rivers, 2001), pp. 183–86.

33. *Ibid.*, p. 188.

34. *Ibid.*, p. 189.

35. Sigmund Freud, "The Interpretation of Dreams," in *The Standard Edition of the Complete Psychological Works of Sigmund Freud, Volume IV (1900): The Interpretation of Dreams (Part I)* (1900), pp. 4–5, PEP Web.

36. Entertainment Software Association, "Essential Facts About the Computer and Video Game Industry," 2017, theesa.com/wp-content/uploads/2017/09/EF2017_Design_FinalDigital.pdf.

37. Simon Parkin, "Zoe Quinn's Depression Quest," *The New Yorker*, September 9, 2014, newyorker.com/tech/elements/zoe-quinnsdepression-quest.

38. Zoe Quinn, Patrick Lindsey, and Isaac Schankler, *Depression Quest*, depressionquest.com.

Chapter 4

39. D. W. Winnicott, *Playing and Reality* (New York: Routledge, 2005), pp. 3–4.

40. *Ibid.*, pp. 13–14.

41. Otto Kernberg, "Borderline Personality Organization," *Journal of the American Psychoanalytic Association* 15, no. 3 (July 1967): pp. 641–85.

42. Peter Fonagy, "Attachment and Borderline Personality Disorder," *Journal of the American Psychoanalytic Association* 48, no. 4 (August 2000): pp. 1129–46.

43. Camilo J. Ruggero et al., "Borderline personality disorder and the misdiagnosis of bipolar disorder," *Journal of Psychiatric Research* 44, no. 6 (April 2010): pp. 405–8.

44. Winnicott, *Playing and Reality*, pp. 55–63.

Chapter 5

45. Jon Peterson, *Playing at the World* (San Diego, California: Unreason, 2012), pp. 595–605.

46. Lawrence Kutner and Cheryl K. Olson, *Grand Theft Childhood* (New York: Simon & Schuster, 2008), pp. 5–28.

47. Brad E. Sheese and William G. Graziano, "Deciding to Defect: The Effects of Videogame Violence on Cooperative Behavior," *Psychological Science* 16, no. 5 (2005): pp. 354–57.

48. *Ibid.*, p. 356.

49. *Ibid.*, p. 356.

50. American Psychological Association, "Resolution on Violence in Videogames and Interactive Media," adopted August 2005, archived August 2015, apa.org/about/policy/interactivemedia.pdf.

51. Christopher J. Ferguson, "The School Shooting/Violent Videogame Link: Causal Relationship or Moral Panic?," *Journal of Investigative Psychology and Offender Profiling* 5 (2008): pp. 25–37.

52. "Scholars" Open Statement to the APA Task Force on Violent Media, September 26, 2013, christopherjferguson.com/APA%20Task%20Force%20Comment1.pdf.

53. American Psychological Association, "Resolution on Violent Videogames," adopted August 2015, apa.org/about/policy/violent-video-games.aspx.

54. "Trump Condemns White Supremacy but Stops Short of Major Gun Controls," Michael Crowley and Maggie Haberman, *The New York Times,* August 5, 2019, nytimes.com/2019/08/05/us/politics/trump-speech-mass-shootings-dayton-el-paso.html.

55. A. Scott Cunningham, Benjamin Engelstätter, and Michael R. Ward, "Understanding the Effects of Violent Video Games on Violent Crime," April 7, 2011, SSRN, papers.ssrn.com/sol3/papers.cfm?abstract_id=1804959.

56. Michael R. Ward, "Videogames and crime," *Contemporary Economic Policy* 29, no. 2 (2011): pp. 261–73.

57. Kutner and Olson, *Grand Theft Childhood,* p. 112.

58. *Ibid.,* p. 114.

59. *Ibid.,* pp. 115–37.

60. *Ibid.,* pp. 195–99.

61. Marie E. Rueve and Randon S. Welton, "Violence And Mental Illness," *Psychiatry (Edgmont)* 5, no. 5 (May 2008): pp. 34–48.

Chapter 6

62. Nick Yee, "Beyond 50/50: Breaking Down the Percentage of Female Gamers by Genre," Quantic Foundry, January 19, 2017, quanticfoundry.com/2017/01/19/femalegamers-by-genre.

63. World Health Organization, "Gaming disorder," *International Classification of Diseases Eleventh Revision,* 2018, icd.who.int/browse11/l-m/en#/http://id.who.int/icd/entity/1448597234.

64. American Psychiatric Association, "Internet Gaming Disorder: A New Phenomenon," 2013, psychiatry.org/File%20Library/Psychiatrists/Practice/DSM/APA_DSM-5- Internet-Gaming-Disorder.pdf.

65. Aarseth Espen et al., "Scholars' open debate paper on the World Health Organization *ICD-11* Gaming Disorder proposal," *Journal of Behavioral Addictions* 6, no. 3 (December 2016): doi.org/10.1556/2006.5.2016.088.

66. Matt Silverman, "25 *Minecraft* Creations That Will Blow Your Flippin' Mind," Mashable, February 13, 2013, mashable.com/2013/02/13/amazingminecraft-creations.

Chapter 7

67. Janet Malcolm, *The Journalist and the Murderer* (New York: Vintage, 1990), pp. 122–23.

68. "Sometimes a Cigar Is Just a Cigar," Quote Investigator, August 12, 2011, quoteinvestigator.com/2011/08/12/just-acigar.

Chapter 8

69. Sigmund Freud, *Civilization and Its Discontents* (London: Penguin, 2004), translated by David McLintock.

70. *Ibid.,* p. 2.

71. Jean-Paul Sartre, *Being and Nothingness; an Essay on Phenomenological Ontology* (New York: Washington Square Press, 1966).

72. Rollo May, *Man's Search For Himself,* (Oxford, England: W. W. Norton, 1953).

73. Freud, *Civilization,* p. 105.

74. "EVE Online From CCP Games, Reykjavik, Iceland," World Summit Awards, 2013, worldsummitawards.org/winner/eve-online-from-ccpgames-reykjavik-iceland.

75. Gameranx, "10 *EVE Online* Facts You Probably Didn't Know," YouTube, March 23, 2017, youtube.com/watch?v=Shhhn6lu0Nc.

76. "EVE Online Wins World Summit Award," *Eve Online* forums, accessed July 20, 2018, forumsarchive.eveonline.com/message/6895324.

77. Steven Messner, "How a scam in *EVE Online* turned into its greatest rescue mission," *PC Gamer,* April 7, 2017, pcgamer.com/how-ascam-in-eve-online-turnedinto-its-greatest-rescuemission.

78. *Ibid.*

79. Wilfred Bion, *Experiences in Groups* (New York: Routledge, 2003), Kindle.

80. *Ibid.,* chap. 4.

81. *Ibid.,* chap. 7.

82. "Riot Games: Assessing toxicity in the workplace," re:Work, accessed July 20, 2018, rework.withgoogle.com/casestudies/riot-games-assessingtoxicity.

83. Cecilia D'Anastasio, *"Inside the Culture of Sexism at Riot Games,"* *Kotaku,* August 7, 2018, kotaku.com/inside-theculture-of-sexism-at-riotgames-1828165483.

Chapter 9

84. Sigmund Freud, "Mourning and Melancholia," in *The Standard Edition of the Complete Psychological Works of Sigmund Freud, Volume XIV (1914–1916): On the History of the Psychoanalytic Movement, Papers on Metapsychology and Other Works* (1917), pp. 237–258, PEP Web.

85. Ernest Becker, *The Denial of Death* (New York: Free Press, 1973).

Chapter 10

86. Matt Perez, "Report: Esports To Grow Substantially And Near Billion-Dollar Revenues In 2018," *Forbes,* February 21, 2018, forbes.com/sites/mattperez/2018/02/21/report-esports-to-growsubstantially-and-near-abillion-dollar-revenuesin-2018.

87. Jason M. Bailey, "School Shooting Simulation Trains Teachers for the Worst," *The New York Times,* February 1, 2018, nytimes.com/2018/02/01/us/schoolshooting- simulation.html.

88. Eberly College of Arts and Sciences, West Virginia University, "Videogames offer active military, veterans coping mechanism for stress," ScienceDaily, accessed July 11, 2018, sciencedaily.com/releases/2017/06/170622122756.

About the Author

Alexander Kriss, PhD, is a clinical psychologist and author. He received his doctorate from The New School for Social Research and completed internship training at Columbia University Medical Center. In 2015, Dr. Kriss opened a private practice in New York City, where he provides psychoanalytic and existential psychotherapy to adolescents and adults dealing with a wide range of issues. He currently serves as an adjunct professor of psychology at the City College of New York and Fordham University, and as a clinical associate at the Safran Center for Psychological Services. Dr. Kriss's writing has appeared in *Kill Screen, Logic,* and numerous academic books and journals. He is the recipient of a University in Exile Fellowship from The New School and a Scholar Award from the Society for Psychoanalysis and Psychoanalytic Psychology. *The Gaming Mind* is his first book.

AlexKriss.com | @alexmkriss